William Digby, National Liberal Federation

Indian Problems for English Consideration

A letter to the Council of the National liberal federation

William Digby, National Liberal Federation

Indian Problems for English Consideration
A letter to the Council of the National liberal federation

ISBN/EAN: 9783337301996

Printed in Europe, USA, Canada, Australia, Japan

Cover: Foto ©Suzi / pixelio.de

More available books at **www.hansebooks.com**

INDIAN PROBLEMS

FOR

ENGLISH CONSIDERATION.

A LETTER

TO THE COUNCIL OF

The National Liberal Federation.

BY

WILLIAM DIGBY, C.I.E.,

HONORARY MEMBER OF THE COBDEN CLUB; HONORARY SECRETARY OF THE INDIAN
FAMINE RELIEF FUND, 1877-78; AUTHOR OF "THE FAMINE CAMPAIGN IN SOUTHERN
INDIA, 1876-78;" "FORTY YEARS IN A CROWN COLONY;" EDITOR OF THE "WESTERN
DAILY MERCURY," ETC.

PUBLISHED FOR THE NATIONAL LIBERAL FEDERATION.

1881.

TO THE COUNCIL OF THE NATIONAL LIBERAL FEDERATION.

GENTLEMEN,,

In the pages of this Letter it is my object to bring Object of Letter. before you—and, through you, the English public—a few facts with reference to the people of India and their country, with the hope that your organisation may become helpful in bring- ing about those reforms which shall make it possible for our Indian fellow-subjects to work out their own advancement with well-grounded confidence and certainty. Lord North- brook, speaking at Birmingham some time ago, remarked, Our Duty to- wards India. 'There is one simple test which we may safely apply to all Indian questions. Let us never forget that it is our duty to govern India, not for our own profit and advantage, but for the benefit of the natives of India.' We, as a nation, are not now acting upon that principle. We err, through ignorance rather than from ill-intent. I know of no organisation so well able to properly instruct and guide the English people in rightly understanding and wisely assisting the inhabitants of India, in the way of free government, than that which you direct. It goes without saying that, in advanced Liberals, the Indian Reform a Liberal duty. Indian people find their best friends. Practically, all that has been done in the Commons' House of Parliament for India has been done by men whom the Federation delights to honour—by, for example—such a man as John Bright, whose efforts to uplift India are approved by the Party of which he is a trusted leader. On the other hand, such means as would infuse native life and vigour into the currents of Indian national and local administration have been opposed by Conservatives, of whom the late Lord Lytton was a typical instance. That noble Lord, when in the House of Commons, deprecated the consideration of Indian questions by that assembly, for this reason : Our doings in India, he said, were often of so doubtful a nature that English freedom would be corrupted by too-familiar acquaintance with the course of proceedings in the empire.* It is, therefore, in accordance with the fitness of things that my attempt to direct the attention of my countrymen to the condition of our fellow-subjects in India should be made through the National Liberal Federation.

Indian Government contrary to English Freedom.

In India, Great Britain possesses a larger Ireland. The proportion is as two hundred and fifty to five : India has two hundred and fifty millions of inhabitants ; Ireland a little over five millions. Probably before the present century has passed away the British people will find themselves face to face in India with difficulties like those which, in connection with Ireland, have caused much trouble and concern during the past fifty years, culminating in the block of legislation which marked the Session of the House of Commons in 1881, when —unfortunate, but necessary, combination—the twin efforts of coercion and amelioration were being carried out. The state of things which, economically, has worked great woe in Ireland exists in a larger degree in India : far more mischief is thereby worked than the people of this country have any conception of. This is patent to an unprejudiced observer ; it is plain and unmistakable even to official apologists. If the Indian official lives who might be expected to prophesy smooth things of India's future, Mr. W. W. Hunter, C.I.E., LL.D., of the Bengal Civil Service, the compiler of the *Imperial Gazetteer of India*, and author of a number of valuable works on the Empire, is that official. In the pages of his books is to be found the

India a larger Ireland.

Official utterances furnish defects of British Rule.

---

* The occasion when this remark was made was the debate in the House of Commons, on the transference of India from "John Company" to the Crown. Lord (then Sir E. Bulwer) Lytton said :—"For my own part, I own to a wholesome dread of hon. gentlemen cramming themselves with blue books, and coming down to the House with an elaborate speech about Rajahs and Nawabs, conceived in accordance with the respective interests of Party ; sometimes, as the case may be, to defend some more than ordinary act of duplicity by which we had annexed a kingdom, or, on the other hand, to declaim against some measure which might be necessary to the stern necessities of oriental rule, but painful to the feelings of an English popular assembly." Injustice . . . painful to the feelings of Englishmen !

strongest possible condemnation of our rule. As I shall show later on, Mr. Hunter, who is regarded as holding a brief for the British Administration, and who is recognised as a most able advocate, is constrained, by the force of the facts with which he has to deal, to make most damaging statements respecting the present condition, and future prospects, of India.

To those who desire that such reforms shall be carried out in India as will tend to remove, at least, the grosser evils of our rule, the testimony of such an authority is of the utmost value. It has become an article of belief in some influential quarters that Indian officials cannot err ; when, therefore, we find in their statement of the case for India ample justification for action, the course is greatly cleared. The time has arrived when the actual facts regarding our Administration should be known. It is a matter of no small importance that the people of India are opening their eyes to the condition of things at present existing. More than that, without any particular ill-will to the British authority, they are threatening stormy weather in the near future. Year by year we are educating, to the highest English standard, hundreds of thousands of Indian youths. A fair percentage of these prove exceptionally well-fitted to take part in the affairs of their country. They are acquainted with the history of their own land, as well as that of other nations, and have sufficient courage to enable them to say those things which they believe to be just, and, in a constitutional manner, to struggle for the attainment of what they consider to be their rights. They do not find, from the point of view of the son of the soil, their country all that could be desired, and they are not prepared contentedly to acquiesce in the continuance of the present state of things. To them, as they regard India, Pope's well-known line is emphatically untrue : they do not believe,

> " Whatever is, is best."

What the leaders of the Land League have been in Ireland, the men we are now educating will be in India, unless the occasion for agitation is removed. The supremely wise course for adoption in regard to India is always to anticipate

[margin notes: Indian Officials cannot err. — Indian Education : probable effects. — Indian Land Leaguers of the future.]

agitation, and, by easy steps, to lead the people into the enjoy-ment of the larger liberty which, almost unconsciously to themselves, they are yearning for, and which, assuredly, their country needs.

ıfferings of the people. Over and above the bad condition of India, from the philosopher's and economist's position, are the ever-present and terrible sufferings which the people have, year by year, to endure. There is nothing in Ireland—notwithstanding Colonel ('Chinese') Gordon's statement that he had seen as great misery in the cabins of Connemara as anywhere in Asia or Africa—to compare with the want and distress in which millions of Indians live from the days of their infancy to the time when the funeral pyre is lighted over their remains, or their bodies are laid in shallow graves. Although the Indians are a patient and long-suffering race, there is a limit even to their patience. When the agitation, which threatens, really comes, it will be largely fed by the sore suffering and misery of these half-starved multitudes.

Trouble ahead India. Nothing that is still unaccomplished can be more certain than that—unless a radical change in administration happens—there is great trouble ahead for the English rulers of India. Common prudence would, therefore, demand that we should take such steps as it may be in our power to take to remove the occasions for disaffection, and to ease the inevitable strain. But higher reasons than those of mere prudence may, and should, guide us. We have, of our own motion and unasked, assumed the responsibility of governing the peoples of India, and must so acquit ourselves that the maximum of good attainable, and not the minimum of accidental advantage, when our own ends have been served, shall be the resultant. It is my belief—a belief born of intimate friend-ship with many Indians of all classes in their own country— How trouble ay be averted. that much of the evil which now impends may be averted, if Englishmen and Indians can be brought to know one another better, and to understand each other's position to a fuller extent than they now do. It is with the hope of doing something towards bringing about, in however humble a measure, such an understanding, that this Letter is written, and that the attention of the National Liberal Federation is directed towards some of the more important features of Indian political and social life. Even the most busy of English statesmen and English men of business can, if they will, devote some attention to Indian affairs. Proof of this is to be found in the interest which Mr. Bright, for many years, has shown in India. There have, in recent times, been few busier men in the United Kingdom than the right hon. gentleman. Yet he has been able to thoroughly acquaint himself with India and its real needs. This was indicated twenty-three years ago, in the speeches which he delivered in the House of Commons in 1858 and 1859, when the Indian Bills of those years were under discussion. Those speeches revealed so complete a mastery of the essentials of Indian politics, that, in so far as Indian reform progresses towards a satisfactory basis, it will be found that it does so on the lines laid down by Mr. Bright when our Eastern Empire passed under the direct dominion of the Crown. *Mr. Bright's interest in India.*

I venture to hope that the presentation of facts in this Letter, and the observations which are founded thereupon, will lead those who are not insensible to the responsibilities we bear towards India to realise that our fellow-subjects in the East are like-minded with ourselves in all that constitutes good citizenship and law-abidingness. This should lead to the opinion that the same principles of procedure which have brought prosperity and contentment to us—though those principles may be varied in their mode of working—will ensure like prosperity and contentment to Indians also. If, in any degree, the middle wall of partition which prevents the one race understanding the other were broken down, or if a breach only were made in it, much would be achieved that would serve to prevent calamities in the future that otherwise must occur. England and India are linked together: it is, above all things, desirable there should be a good understanding between their respective inhabitants. *Good points in Indian character*

I.—THE PEOPLE OF INDIA AS THEY ARE.

Point of view
in   estimating
Indians.

IN estimating the character of a people, very much depends upon the point of view from which they are regarded. For example, in the month of June last, a disturbance, in which certain American runners were hustled, occurred on the running grounds at Aston, a few miles from Birmingham. Immediately, the cry was raised in certain metropolitan Conservative papers, ' See, these are the people who send Mr. Bright and Mr. Chamberlain to Parliament! This is Democracy! These be your gods, oh! Radical Englishmen!' Arguing from the conduct of a few roughs, who may or may not have belonged to Birmingham, the writers in the papers referred to, because they dislike the political proclivities of the great midland town, stigmatized the whole population as ruffians. They described the Birmingham people generally in terms applicable only to a few individuals 'of the baser sort,' whose identity with Birmingham was not proved. The same principle is too often acted upon in descriptions of the character of the inhabitants of India. You question two men who have lived in the country about its peoples. One declares them to be 'niggers,'—the wonder will be if he does not say 'damned niggers,'—utterly untrustworthy, and very low in the scale of civilization, in fact, altogether beneath the notice of an Englishman. The other, on the contrary, will declare that Indian folk are very commendable folk indeed ; that he has found true and hearty friends among them ; that he believes them, if fairly treated, capable of filling an important place among the peoples of the world. The one observer looks for defects, and finds defects, which, no doubt, exist in some degree, but he sees defects only ; the other is not blind to defects, but he is more anxious to see good qualities than bad, and, as a necessary consequence, good qualities are displayed towards him.

Contradictory
descriptions.

I am glad to be able to testify that my experience of *Personal testi-mony.* Indians has been of the latter kind. I found the Indians with whom I came into contact during my residence in the East— and I had peculiar opportunities, from a combination of circumstances, arising out of my famine relief and journalistic duties, of knowing intimately many of all ranks and conditions—men whom it was a pleasure to know, men with whom it was a privilege to work. If I could but make them known to Englishmen in any degree as they really are, I should be very glad, for I am satisfied my countrymen would then see that the people of India were worthy of any trouble which their fellow-subjects in Great Britain might take on their behalf. If I do not succeed in persuading some to take a great deal of trouble on behalf of our Indian friends, then this Letter will have been written in vain : the object I have in view will fail in its accomplishment. When, a hundred years ago, the *An incident at Arcot.* fort of Arcot, in Southern India, was besieged by the French, English and Madras troops were shut up together. Provisions ran short ; famine stared the garrison in the face. At length, when the worst came to the worst, and scarcely any food remained, the Madras Sepoys begged that their European comrades would eat the rice provided for the daily meal, while they would be content with the water in which it was boiled. The Sepoys urged that Englishmen, in an unaccustomed climate, needed more sustenance than did they who were ' to the climate born,' and were better able to bear tropical privation. The story is typical. It is not an isolated or accidental incident. An Indian, whatever his caste, or creed, or nationality, delights to manifest respect towards Europeans, when the latter prove themselves worthy of regard. Surely English electors can spare a little time for effort on behalf of such a people as this, and are ready to attempt those reforms which shall lead the people of India to a better and more self-respecting position than they now occupy.

I know that the ordinary European in India looks upon *Ordinary ideas of Indians.* the natives he has to do with, or of whom he hears now and again, as exceptionally stupid. But I also remember that

Cardinal Newman has remarked, in his own incomparable manner, that mankind generally has described the lion as a pusillanimous beast. Possibly, the lion might say that man was cowardly if it were able to describe some of the bipeds with whom it had dealings, how, through fear of a lion, they ran to places of safety, where they could be secure from its strength and courage. The second day after I landed in Ceylon, the gentleman with whom I was staying said, of the people generally, 'If it is possible to do a thing wrongly, they will do it. Now, mark that coolie! You will find that he puts your box with its front to the wall.' Sure enough, the coolie did so. If I had been a passing visitor to the East, as, for instance, Mr. Anthony Trollope was to Ceylon a few years ago, I might have gone away with notions as erroneous respecting the people as he did regarding the island generally—erroneous observations which, by a system of co-operative journalism, were circulated over the greater part of the United Kingdom.

Population. There are over two hundred and fifty millions of people in India. Ninety per cent. are engaged in agricultural operations, either as small landowners— to be exact, as tenants with fixity of tenure, and occupancy rights in the soil they cultivate,—or as labourers. Their condition is so wretched that it has been declared by one who is at present occupying a high administrative position in India that at least half of those engaged in agriculture do not know what it is, from year's end to year's end, to have their appetite thoroughly satisfied. The most favourable present-day picture of India, viz., that by Dr. Hunter, in his pamphlet, 'England's Work in India,' and in his Gazetteer, reveals the terrible fact that **Forty millions** FORTY MILLIONS OF PEOPLE ARE INSUFFICIENTLY FED,* **of hungry people** *i.e.*, are in a state of continual semi-starvation. In ten years, as Mr. Caird, C.B., has pointed out, the forty millions will

---

* "England's Work in India," by W. W. Hunter, C.I.E., LL.D., p. 80. " . . . . The remaining fifth, or forty millions, go through life on insufficient food."

have become sixty millions—(the land is becoming exhausted, inferior soils are coming into cultivation). In a word, nearly twice as many people as there exist of all classes in the United Kingdom are daily starving in India. Will Englishmen, *can* Englishmen, contemplate such a condition of things without making heroic efforts to render its continuance impossible?

That the pressure upon the population of India must of necessity be great will be apparent when the density of population per square mile is considered. In British India there are 211 persons to the square mile. It will be readily seen that, in a country which has practically no manufactures—(there were manufactories in India once, but in that land, as in Ireland, we, in our beneficence, have killed native manufacturing enterprise)—the struggle for life must be most severe. It was discovered, by the Famine Commissioners in 1879, that, in a portion of Bengal, allowing for women and children, a population of twenty-four millions were struggling to live upon fifteen millions of acres, or a little more than half-an-acre each. *Density of population*

To continue the comparison with England: Forty-two per cent., or nearly half the British population, live in towns of twenty thousand inhabitants and upwards. In India only one-twentieth of the population reside in towns. Trustworthy authority says, 'Whenever the numbers of a people exceed one to the acre, or 640 to the square mile, except in suburban districts, or in irrigated tracts, the struggle for existence becomes hard. At half-an-acre a-piece the struggle is very hard. In such districts a good harvest yields just sufficient food for the people; and thousands of lives depend each autumn on a few inches, more or less, of rainfall. The Government may, by great efforts, feed the starving in time of actual famine; but it cannot stop the yearly work of disease and death among *a steadily underfed people.*' * *Population chiefly agricultural.*

---

* Imperial Gazetteer of India (Trubner & Co., London), vol. iv., p. 169.

An underfed people.

'A STEADILY UNDERFED PEOPLE!' This is one of the facts I wish my fellow-countrymen could apprehend : I am confident they would not, if they realised the truth, be content to let things run their course without an attempt at amelioration. There should be no mistaking the full meaning of the expressions I have quoted. On official estimates,— which always err on the favourable side, which always minimise (unconsciously, no doubt) such facts as I am dealing with,—*one person in every six in India is in a condition of gradual starvation*, and this through no fault of his own. In addition, consider also this farther fact, viz., that, during the past twenty years, nearly half-a-million persons per annum, on an average, have died in India from absolute want of food. The particulars are as follow :—

Millions starved to death

		Deaths.
Famine in Upper India, 1861		500,000
,, Orissa, Behar, and N. Madras, 1866		1,500,000
,, Rajputana and Central India, 1869		400,000
,, Southern India and Bombay, 1876-1877 ...		5,500,000
,, North-West Provinces, 1877		750,000

8,650,000

Again, I would remark that these are the official statements, and that they err from under-, rather than from over-, statement.

People steadily growing poor.

Another important feature of the existing state of affairs in India, brought about under our rule, if not actually as the result of the course of government we adopt, deserves special prominence. The people are, year by year, steadily growing poorer, and the possibility of earning a livelihood is becoming increasingly hard. In the large towns and near the railways, new occupations have sprung into existence which find employment for thousands, but even here the increase of wages has not kept pace with the increase in the price of food, and life is a perpetual struggle. Proof of the foregoing statements may be given.

In the Madras Presidency, which certainly is not the least efficiently administered part of India, our rule is harder to the people than was the native rule, and is steadily growing worse. In special returns prepared by the Madras Board of Revenue for the Famine Commission, certain details are given respecting the price of food which are pregnant with matter for grave concern. It would seem that since 1814, taking in each case the average of five years from that date, and comparing the first quinquennial period with the last, viz., 1814-1819 with 1870-1874, the cost of second-sort rice has doubled, save and except in the irrigated districts. That is, *while in England the process of the law has had the effect of reducing the price of the staple article of food, and making it cheap and plentiful for every one, the exactly opposite principle has prevailed in India.* This statement is as true of the ' dry-grain ' food—*i.e.*, millet, and the like, as of the ' wet '—*i.e.*, rice. Ragi—a species of dry grain—during the period mentioned, has doubled in price, the number of seers per rupee being, in some cases, 52·6 in 1819-1823, against 35·4 in 1870-1874 ; while the fluctuations have been from 65·5 in 1814 to 16·0 in 1866, and much less than sixteen in the famine years of 1876 and 1877. Again, testing this by an English standard, it is as though the 4-lb. loaf in England had gone up from sixpence to two shillings on exceptional occasions, and had permanently increased to one shilling, without corresponding advantages to the purchaser in the way of larger means of earning money. Indeed, when the prices have been at their highest range, the opportunities for earning money have been the fewest. Cumboo and Cholum, ' dry ' grains largely used by the people, show the same change to a steadily-increasing and permanently-increased price, with the difference, as regards Cholum, that the five years from 1861 to 1865 were the worst in the returns before me as I write. The returns for the period from 1875 to 1880 are available ; they show that period to have been the most severe for a century. Old people among the Indians say that food is dearer now than it was in their younger

Increasing cost of food.

Compared with English prices.

Old times, good times. days. Unfortunately, the remark does not partake of that untrustworthy optimism of most old people—that the good times were the old times; official records support the former contention. It is true that, as regards the labourer, high prices do not affect him so much as they would do if he were always paid in money. But, as is well remarked by a writer in the official document upon which these observations are based, 'When prices are high as the result of failure of crop, and the employer himself becomes embarrassed, the position even of the permanent agricultural servant becomes critical. Having been unable to save anything to stand him in stead in time of need, and there being no demand for service elsewhere, he is thrown entirely on private or public charity for means of subsistence.' In the Madras Presidency alone, reckoning those dependent upon a labourer as being a wife and only one child—saying nothing of aged parents unable to work, who are tended with an affection truly admirable— there are eight millions of persons in this unfortunate condition. As all Hindus marry, and as the average number in a family is four, it will be seen that the above estimate of the extent of suffering in the landless and insufficiently-fed class is extremely moderate.

Buying power not increasing. From almost every part of the Empire the same story comes, but it is not necessary that I should burden these pages with more details of this character. The cost of food to the common people has risen greatly; wages have not increased in the same proportion. Life, I repeat, is yearly growing harder to our unfortunate fellow-subjects: the horizon of hope is contracting; their misery is increasing.

Rice not the only food. It may be mentioned, partly by way of clearing up a misconception which largely prevails in this country, that the food of the people of India is not, as is generally supposed, exclusively rice. An idea to the contrary is current, chiefly perhaps, because irrigation works are frequently recommended as a panacea against famine. Upon that point—*i.e.*, the value of irrigation works as one out of a number of means to be used as a preventive of famine—I shall have something to say later on. Meanwhile, I may remark that the rice-eating population of India is only one-third of the whole. Examining by Presidencies and Provinces, it will appear that in Madras, where—next to British Burma—the largest quantity of rice is grown, the area under this 'wet crop' is 33 per cent. of the whole acreage cultivated ; in Bombay, the area is 10 per cent. ; in Sind, 17 per cent. ; in the Central Provinces, 34 per cent. ; and in the Panjab, 5 per cent. In none of the Native States is rice grown to any large extent. The general food of those people is wheat or millets, known generally as ragi, cholum, or jowari.

General food wheat or millet.

What is the character of the people whose means of existence are so precarious, who suffer so severely ? There are not more law-abiding, contented, and, on the whole, lovable races under the wide sway of the Queen than the people of India. These good qualities, however, are not developed from the comfort of their surroundings, but exist in spite of misery which might be expected to render goodness impossible. Their worldly possessions are of the slightest value. Their poverty is so acute that English people can scarcely realise it. Save that, in the agricultural districts, there is no over-crowding—the kindly climate making it possible to sleep in the open air—no Dorsetshire or Devonshire labourer's dwelling can be compared with the wretchedness of the Indian labourer's 'home.' Further, in England the dilapidated and miserable cottages are the exception ; in India, for many millions, they are the rule. Save and except in towns, where civilisation has created the need, and where trade supplies the means for gratifying it, Indian homes have few evidences of what we regard as comfort. Even in regard to those whose incomes raise them above want, tiled houses are rarely seen, and masonry walls are still more rare. Mud walls, the same inside as outside, and thatched roofs, are the rule. The rooms have no ceiling, the walls no sort of ornament or decoration, and the floor is

The character of the people, law abiding and contented.

Miserable homes.

of simple earth, beaten hard. There is nothing of what is commonly called furniture. There are no chairs, or tables, or couches, or beds; the people, for the most part, sleep on the earthen floor, with only a mat or a small cotton carpet beneath them. As I have said, the foregoing description applies to ryots, who may be called well-to-do. Of the labourers, who are to be counted by millions, a very much worse story has to be told. Practically, all their earnings go for food, or are paid in food; the wretched hut in which the labourer lives can scarcely be valued at all. Says one who came very closely into contact with the people during an epidemic of cholera :—' It was then I first really learned the poverty of the agricultural classes. Sometimes I had four or five patients in the same house; and not a spare rag in the house more than the inmates had on their persons, and not more than a few days' food.'

Labourers earnings mostly paid in food.

The poverty of the Indians, and the fact that a little money goes a very long way among them, were shown in a marked manner in the vast amount of good accomplished through the fund of nearly £800,000, contributed by England and the colonies during 1877 and 1878, for the famine-stricken of that period, who were not reached by the means provided by the Government. From that sum nearly nine-and-a-half-millions of meals were provided; or partial sustenance for a week at a time was granted during the severest period of the distress, by the gift of eight annas (one shilling) to applicants whose need had been tested. More than one hundred and forty-four thousand houses were repaired or rebuilt at an average cost of six shillings each. It is matter for gratification that so much could be done with the money; but, on the other hand, it is a distressing thought that the value of an ordinary dwelling should be considerably less than one pound sterling. Yet another form of charity disbursed from the fund in question was that which, literally, set up in business men who had been completely ruined. Nearly half-a-million of cultivators received assistance, in the shape of

Modes of relief in famine.

Food.

Rebuilding Houses.

Helping cultivators.

seed for sowing, the pay of hiring bullocks to plough the land, and for like operations ; all this was done at a cost of less than ten shillings each individual, taking the average. In a similar way, poor artizans were started afresh. A few shillings for Assisting Arti-zans. the purchase of yarn or other materials for weaving, or the redemption of a loom which had been pawned when food was dearest and most scarce, sufficed to raise a weaver from beggary to a decent position in life. A quarter of a million people of this class were helped at an average of four shillings each. Probably, by these statements, Englishmen will be able to gather some idea of the utter poverty of the Indian people. It is true that the necessities of their position are not so great as those of corresponding classes in this country ; but when full allowance is made on that score, the condition of things remaining is terrible.

The patience of the men and women with whom we have Wonderful patience of the people. to do is wonderful. During ordinary periods there is far less crime among them than among people similarly situated in any European country. But it is in times of sore distress, when food is five times above its normal price, and not easy to get then, that their patience is truly sublime. Take their conduct during the awful times of 1876 and 1877 : They saw their crops perish before their eyes, and did not consider that they must wreak vengeance upon their rulers, or in any way disturb the public peace ; they were starving, but not one in a hundred thousand resorted to robbery ; it was the exception, not the rule, to hear of grain-carts being looted. On the beach, at Madras, a few hungry folk might be seen making holes in the bags of rice as they were being carted, and gathering the grains which fell. On the whole, however, the terrible affliction was borne with exemplary conduct. The district judge at Trichinopoly (Mr. E. Forster Webster), speaking of people whose sense of self-respect would not allow them to attend a Government relief camp, said, ' The closer you look into matters, and the better you know the people, the more you see how fearfully widely spread is the present distress, borne by the poor creatures in dumb

B

resignation to fate, and with scarcely a murmur.' Had they not been thus patient, had they proved as restless as the English people would have been, were they situated in like circumstances, the possibility of maintaining our supremacy in Southern India and in Bombay would, in all probability, have been decided against us.

Kindliness towards each other. Again, as to their kindliness towards one another. The famine gave wonderful proof of the depth and sincerity of this quality. We saw it in our own homes, in the privations our servants endured, that they might be able to help their friends who had no work; we met with numerous instances in our offices, where the *employés* visibly grew thinner and more woe-begone day by day, the higher wages given by employers going to support relatives in greater need than those by whom increased pay was received. One native member of the Central Famine Committee said to me one day, ' I have thirty-five people depending upon me for daily food.' It was a common experience in our Relief Camps and in our Day Nurseries to note that the people did not struggle with one another as to who should be first served ; it seemed as if the rule was, the greater the need of the individual the greater the goodness and the patience displayed. 'Mothers, aunts, grandmothers, or neighbours,' said one diligent worker in the cause of relief, who had medical oversight of a Day Nursery, 'will bring children to be fed, and, though in want themselves, never express, by word or sign, a desire to share in the help they know is meant only for young children. Big boys will bring little boys, and, though lank and hungry, and casting longing eyes on food, are only intent on seeing that their charges get their allotted ration. For six weeks past a little girl of ten or eleven has been bringing up two sickly children twice a day, nursing them with the tenderest care, and never asking bite or sup on her own account. She showed no signs of starvation until the last few days, when I noticed that she was beginning to go down, and I have asked the lady of the Nursery to bring her on the list of those to whom one good meal a day may mean the salvation of life.' The gratitude, too, for the help rendered and the sympathy shown, was of a most marked character.

As regards personal conduct, general abstinence, and the like, the Indian people of the lower classes are, if not all that could be desired, at least far better than those in other countries. They do not consume intoxicating drinks, save, perhaps, at the annual religious festival, and even then sparingly. In the 'glad riot' of the one holiday in the year their conduct is orderly, if tested by a Western standard, and their abstemiousness beyond all praise. Their substance, such as it is, is not wasted in riotous living. Nor do they encourage the sale of intoxicants. When Village Communities, having authority within their jurisdiction to impose fines and sentence to imprisonment, were revived in one portion of our rule in the East, and the villagers were summoned to make bye-laws for the guidance of affairs, they passed regulations which forbad the sale of liquor, or ganja, or opium, while they prohibited bullock-hackery racing on the high road. * Local Option has, with them, the effect which Sir Wilfrid Lawson and the United Kingdom Alliance believe it will have in Great Britain and Ireland, when Parliament has sanctioned its adoption. It is a sad fact, however, that the

Habits and general conduct very good. Few drunkards.

---

* Among the rules of these Village Communities are some which may be quoted. Their good sense will doubtless astonish some whose ideas of orientals are gathered from wrong notions which have been too long current :—*e.g.*, "7. At the request, by petition, of the parents or guardians of twenty-five or more children for the establishment of a school, a school shall be established, which is to be built at the expense of all the villagers within two miles of the proposed school : provided, always, that a schoolmaster is provided without charge to the villagers [*i.e.*, at the cost of the Government]. The repair and upkeep of the school-house or room shall be provided for by the levy of a moderate fee from the pupils attending the school, or by labour given gratuitously by the parents or guardians of such children. *Any parent who does not send his children to either the village school or any other place of education shall be considered as totally unfit for holding any office under Government, or of being a member of a Gansabhawa* " (Village Council).

"Boys from six to fifteen years old, and girls from six to twelve years old, shall be sent to school by their parents or guardians, except when prevented by sickness or other material cause ; and the parents or guardians infringing this rule shall be subject to a fine not exceeding one rupee."

"13. No cart-racing shall be permitted upon any public road, and no vehicle shall be driven thereon without a light at night."

"14. Gambling and cock-fighting are prohibited. Every headman is requested to prosecute offenders against this rule before the Village Tribunal, as also all disorderly persons and vagrants, also persons using obscene and abusive language."

Another rule prohibits pawning articles " without notice previously given to the village headman."—(From (" A Home Rule Experiment in Ceylon," by Wm. Digby, *Fortnightly Review*, August, 1875.)

good sense of the Indian people, in regard to intoxicants, is being overborne by considerations of revenue, and that, for the sake of the money obtained from the issue of licenses, grog-shops are encouraged. The Rev. T. Evans, Baptist Missionary at Monghyr, Bengal, finds the state of affairs in that district becoming so bad, through the multiplication of licensed drinking-houses, that he has, twice within the past twelve months, addressed the Viceroy on the subject.

Character of villagers.

'A very happy-natured, contented race, as a whole, are our village husbandmen,' says Mr. Allan Hume, C.B., Secretary of the now defunct Revenue, Agricultural, and Commerce Department in India, 'and they have their little amusements and festivals, and when harvests are good, pretty much all that, with their simple habits, they need. The picture is not all black, or how could we, or anyone, hold the country? But withal, their lives are very hard and toilsome, and through it, all too many are pressed with debt. Good crops ease the pain a little, and the village merry-making brings a temporary forgetfulness, but *the sore is always there, and, except in very good seasons, multitudes, for months in every year, cannot get sufficient food for themselves and their families.* They are not starving, but they are hungry; they get less than they want, and than they ought to have.'

These are the people, forty millions of whom, says Dr. Hunter, speaking with exceptional knowledge and authority, go all their lives without enough food to eat. For their government and well-being English electors are responsible. These are the people whose position ought to be improved, and may be improved if Englishmen and Englishwomen care to take a little trouble on their account.

Higher classes

As for the higher classes, what is their character, what their disposition? Are they worthy of fellowship with Englishmen? Are they deserving of a little self-sacrificing effort on our part, that 'ample space and verge enough' shall be provided, in which they may grow to a proper mental, moral, and political standard? The reader shall judge. Sir

Richard Temple, whose experience of the Indian people has Sir R. Temple on their good been very wide and varied, in his work on ' India in 1880,' qualities. recently published, says ; '. . . . . But with an English-man who lives and labours in the country, the wider his acquaintance with the natives, and the deeper his insight, the greater is his liking for them. He who has the best and longest acquaintance with the natives esteems them most. . . . . . He who has the best data for an opinion regard-ing them, and the firmest ground on which to found his belief, will have the most hopeful faith in their mental and moral progress. . . . . Many of their virtues are of a type or mould different from the Anglo-Saxon, but the domestic qualities shine with a quiet unobtrusive light, which deserves the admiring gaze of even the most civilized nations. . . . There is, in their disposition, a cheerful and courageous patience nurtured in the midst of national tribulations, a willingness to submit the unruly will to the dictates of a venerated law, and a reliance on an Almighty Power as the Refuge of the Weak, and the Helper of the Helpless, which are akin to the best forms of religion.' Herein, we know that Sir Richard testifieth truly. The Indian people, as a whole, are all he describes them to be, and more besides.

In business life, to take another class in the social scale, Indians in Business. the average Indian is as much worthy of commendation, esteem, and trust, as is the agriculturist, with whom we have tarried. All the qualities which lead to success in mercantile affairs in this country are exhibited by the Indian merchant and trader. In the Madras Presidency, many Collectors testify specially to the energy of the Mahommedan traders, and with regard to the Hindu commercial castes, Dr. Cornish, the Compiler of the Census Tables, remarks :—' They have not the whole field to themselves; for many Mahommedans and Hindus of other castes are now competing with them; but they hold their own, as communities possessing capital, gifted with the spirit of enterprise, and free from the vice of personal extravagance, must always do.' ' No merchants in

.he world are more shrewd than those of India,' said Mr. J. B.
Norton, in 1854, in a letter to Lord Sherbrooke, when (as
Robert Lowe) he was Joint Secretary of the Board of Control
of the East India Company. In the more pleasing aspects of
character the business man is not wanting. The garden of an
Culture and charity. Indian merchant, which I visited, with its owner, shortly before
I left India, was as much a matter of pride to him as a tulip
bed was wont to be to a Dutch merchant, or as his greenhouses
are to the average Englishman of to-day. When an Indian
merchant has made money he does not hoard it. On the
contrary, he freely parts with it; he is anxious to disburse it
in charity. The gentleman whose liking for flowers I have
mentioned, during more than twelve months of the Madras
famine fed sixteen hundred people daily in his own compound.
When the distress was overpast he said to me, 'I have been
very prosperous in business, and am anxious to build a lying-in
ward at the Monegar Choultry Hospital; my aged mother,
too, is anxious I should do this before she dies.' The ward
was built at considerable cost and, I believe, has since been
adequately endowed. My friend is not exceptional in the
exhibition of the good qualities I have mentioned. This would
be more often seen by Anglo-Indians if, while they are in
India, they would take the trouble to understand those with
whom they come into contact, and be at some pains to call
forth the best side of the character of those in whose land
Englishmen are mere birds of passage, sojourners for a time.
The mercantile and trading class is active and energetic in
public affairs. Its members contest seats for the Municipal
Councils, and are earnest and devoted in committee work,
whether in the transaction of their own caste affairs, or in
educational or philanthropic effort. There are all the essentials
of a good citizen in each individual of the mercantile and
trading section of the Indian population.

Professional men. Ascending yet a step higher, we come to the professional
men. These, as scholastic professors, barristers, lawyers, and
Government servants, are in no degree behind their country-

men in other ranks of life in exhibiting aspects of character of a praiseworthy kind. Perhaps, I cannot better describe this section of the Indian race than by a brief sketch of one Indian gentleman, whom I knew intimately, and esteemed most highly. He was a Tamil of high caste, and spent, I believe, four years as a student in the Presidency College, Madras. Partly through the example of, and contact with, a relative who had been to Europe more than once, my friend adopted a semi-European dress, and very well it became him too. He was, when in the college, a lad of good natural abilities, but apparently not susceptible to cram, or mere learning by rote ; at least, he did not take a degree at the University. When I first knew him he had left college a few years, and had been sworn as an Advocate of the Supreme Court. I knew nothing then about the rival systems of education in the various Presidencies, but I was induced to form a high opinion of the teaching in Madras from the good effects of it which I saw in my friend R. The result of this scholastic training had been to develop in him a keen desire to extend the horizon of his knowledge after he had left the College. He kept up his reading in the leading philosophic and scientific works of the day, and no man—Englishman or Indian—in the Library to which he belonged was more choice in the selection of books, or read them more diligently or intelligently. This was seen when, after writing a work on ' The Philosophy of Law,' he appended a list of the authors he had consulted, after the manner Henry Buckle made fashionable : my Tamil friend's list was no contemptible one, even when mentioned in the same sentence as Buckle's. Politically he was as active as he was diligent intellectually. I had only known him a few weeks, when I had occasion to attend a town's meeting regarding sanitation, and found that he was a speaker to one of the Resolutions : right well and appropriately did he deal with the topic entrusted to him, speaking fluently from notes, and in good colloquial English. In larger political matters he was greatly interested, when the lead was given him ; for, as he often confessed, he did not feel confidence enough in himself to initiate reforms, but he did feel that he could second anybody else's efforts very vigorously. And, as I happen to be aware, he did so with his purse as well as with his tongue and his pen ; all who know the people of India will agree that the test is a sure one in the East as in the West, that a man's real interest in a cause may be tried by his willingness to give pecuniary assistance to it. This test R. stood admirably. He was also 'diligent in business,' taking up law-reporting in addition to his other duties ; he has published several volumes of reports, volumes which have received the encomiums of the Judges in the Court in which he practises. To the objection which might be urged that my friend was all that I described him to be intellectually, but, morally and spiritually, what is he ? my reply is ready. Though not a professing Christian, R. is as good a man as, or better than, a great many Christians so-called ! Religious topics were, for a time, avoided by both of us, but when men become intimate friends, the barrier of reserve on the chief of all subjects must soon be broken down. It was broken down so far as we were concerned. I found my friend was not a Christian, but just as certainly he was not an Atheist. He believed in God, holding that the Deity whom Christians adored and the Deity on which the super-structure of Hinduism has been reared were in essence the same. He once quoted against me a passage in the Epistle to the Romans, I think, where the writer says that God has in every land those who trust in, and fear, Him, and who, presumably, will be saved. The inspiration of the Scriptures, and the incarnation of Jesus Christ, were things he could not bring himself to believe in, whilst also he could not confess to having experienced that deep and lasting yearning after a greater than one's self (which most men who pass through deep waters experience), in whose wisdom confidence might be reposed. Still, he admitted that might come in time. He was not self-conscious or conceited, and he possessed what are, in Christian parlance, called 'the graces of the Spirit,' for he was sober, not given to frivolous or malicious conversation, ready to think the best of everybody, and yet, withal, courageous in the maintenance of his convictions, proof of the latter quality being given on many occasions when the necessity for a stone-wall stand arose.

That man, my friend R., is the product of English education in India ; I think the product is one of which we have no reason to be ashamed. The gentleman whose character I have faintly outlined is now the nominated representative of his race in a Legislative Council. But for the fear that I should weary the readers of this Letter, I should like, from the seven volumes of Legislative Council Debates which are by my side as I write, to give many illustrations of the capacity and ability of the educated oriental for counsel and debate. Lord Northbrook,* sometime Viceroy of India, now First Lord of the Admiralty, however, shall supply a few facts. His lordship, stating that, in his position as Viceroy, he only came into contact with the educated natives, gave his opinion respecting them. Among them was the late Rajah Romanath Tagore, a member of the Legislative Council of the Viceroy, who often gave the Government most valuable assistance ; and the late Dwarkanath Mitra, who was for six years a Judge of the High Court of Calcutta. ' We, in England,' said Lord Northbrook, 'sometimes forget that the manner in which Indian questions are treated in Parliament and in the Press here is thoroughly understood by the educated natives of India. This attention to English politics is not confined to the educated natives of British territories. At the Native Courts the articles of our English newspapers are habitually translated and read. Dr. Bellew's travels and Sir Henry Rawlinson's essays were studied at the Court of the Amir of Kabul. Moreover, there are newspapers published in India— notably, the *Hindoo Patriot* of Calcutta—written in English, exclusively by natives, which hold their own well with the Anglo-Indian journals.' Englishmen can judge for themselves whether, with men of the kind above described,

Product of English Education generally good.

Lord Northbrook's testimony.

---

* Speech delivered in the Town Hall, Birmingham, in 1879.

increasing in numbers year by year, we shall not have to re-cast our relations with India. Scope must be found for their trained energies and for their legitimate ambition, or they will, in a manner that may be unpleasant to us, find scope for themselves.

Indian states-
men.

There now remains one other class of Indians whom I wish specially to mention. A knowledge of them, and an acquaintance with their work, cannot fail to deepen the respect which the English people should cherish for their fellow-subjects in India. I refer to the statesmen who, in peculiar positions, and with many restraints, have given evidence of the possession of wonderful faculties and marvellous ability. Sir Salar Jung has regenerated the Nizam's Dominions; Sir Madhava Rao has changed decay and chaos in Travancore to prosperity and order, and in Baroda has done equally good work, amid difficulties that were stupendous ; Sir Dinkur Rao ; Mr. Raghunath Rao, Minister to the Maharajah Holkar ; and many others who might be named, have displayed the administrative ability of the Indian in no common degree. The capacity of this group of statesmen, taken singly, may be gauged by a brief recital of what Sir Salar Jung has done in the Deccan—first, for the country whose affairs he has administered in time of plenty and in time of famine ; and, second, in the prudence and patience he has shown in the face of difficulties innumerable, and of insults wellnigh unbearable. Sir Salar Jung's career has been that of a great Reformer, great in the sense in which Englishmen are apt to regard the work of Mr. Gladstone during the late session of Parliament (1881) as great, viz., in masterly and masterful dealing with complicated land questions which strike at the root of the well-being of Society.

Sir Salar Jung
as a Land Re-
former.

This is not the place in which to—nor is it necessary for the purposes of this Letter that I should—take a survey of all Sir Salar Jung's good work as a Reformer. It will suffice if I show what he has done in relation to Land

Reform, chiefly because that is the great rock ahead in Indian administration. That is the feature respecting which, from the time of Lord Cornwallis's gigantic blunder in creating landlords (in the English sense of the term) and in making a permanent settlement, we, as rulers, have been most helpless and most unsuccessful ; and also, because, from the intricacies of the subject, from the local knowledge required, certitude and satisfaction on this important matter will only be obtained by, and through, Indian statesmen. Sir Salar Jung assumed charge of the government of his Highness the Nizam's Dominions in 1853. As soon as he had made himself master of the facts, he took in hand the improvement of the land revenue. He found abuses in plenty existing. Revenue farmers stood between the Government and the peasantry, and became extortioners of the worst class. They invented pretexts for levying taxes which were illegal, and ground down the peasantry almost to powder. The Prime Minister of the Nizam grappled with this evil and conquered it. A measure of his far-sightedness and courage may be gathered when I state that, twenty years after revenue farming had been abolished in the Native State he administered, that infamous system flourished in the colony of Ceylon, which is ruled from Downing-street, and for whose righteous government the English people are directly responsible. Fortunately, a change for the better in some slight degree has been brought about in Ceylon by the adoption of such means as this Letter is intended to call forth., viz., constitutional agitation through the British Parliament.

The difficulties in the way of Sir Salar Jung were stupendous, but he overcame them. Probably, dry details respecting the Sarbastedari system, the Zemindari system, or the Ryotwari principle, are unnecessary. It may suffice if I state that, after the most careful investigation, the Minister decided not to follow Lord Cornwallis's bad example, and create a new class of landlords, though the advantage to an Administration of such a class was not overlooked. The decision which Sir Salar came to was in favour of direct

Revenue farming abolished.

Right in the soil conferred on tenants.

communication between the Government and the tenants, the latter obtaining rights in the soil they cultivated, rights at the mention of which many Members of the British House of Commons would stand aghast, and the contemplation of which would drive Mr. Henry Chaplin to frenzy. In the direction towards which land legislation in Ireland is tending, Sir Salar Jung laboured, with the result that the prosperity of the inhabitants of the Deccan is vastly increased, the State revenues are enormously larger, exactions and impositions are reduced to a minimum, and a degree of general contentment marks his Highness's Dominions, which is not to be found in the larger portion of the British-ruled territory by which those Dominions are surrounded. There is no honour in the keeping of the British Crown too great for the man who performed this task—(if the next Garter that falls vacant were sent to Hyderabad, a right step would be taken) ; but, instead of receiving honour, because Sir Salar Jung, through too-great devotion to his country, is out of favour with the Calcutta Foreign Office, he has been subjected to contumely and insult of a petty and discreditable kind. The story of his treatment, however, cannot find a place here.

Abolition of payment in kind — Sir Salar Jung's third reform in connection with the land was the abolition of payment-in-kind. This is a system vicious in many ways, and objectionable both to the State and to the cultivator. Exact knowledge by the State of the area of the land or of the producibility of the soil is not, under payment-in-kind, a pre-requisite, and is not possessed : all that the State cares about is the quantity of grain produced, of which it claims its portion. Sir Salar Jung's description of the evils of the old mode, contained in a State paper which he furnished to the Famine Commissioners in 1879, is complete in showing the necessity for doing away with that system. The adaptability of native officials to administrative work of a high order was proved by the thorough manner in which a change so great as this and so difficult was simultaneously and peacefully introduced throughout the territory affected. Well-considered rules and energetic effort speedily overcame the obstacles which, at first sight, appeared insurmountable.

These facts, described in barest form, from a wealth of material available, will serve to show the capacity of the Indian mind, and indicate the excellent material which is ready for English thoughtfulness to take in hand, and shape for higher and better things than the mere 'hewing of wood and drawing of water' in which all but a very small portion of that material is now employed. A wider field, larger opportunities, are imperatively needed for the educated and able men of India.

II.—THE COUNTRY AS IT IS.

Effect upon a conquered people of being held in subjection.

IN an ideal world the holding of one country in subjection by another would not be possible. Nor, when that period comes, 'by good men prayed for long,' when the average of goodness and intelligence the world over becomes higher, will such over-rule and subjection continue. Let the intentions of conquerors be never so humane, the necessities of the position which they occupy render it inevitable that—often without knowing it, more often without meaning it—they shall be guilty of oppression, they shall exhibit the vices of arrogance and greed. Everything will be made to give way to the necessities, or supposed necessities, of the superior race, let the cost be what it may. On the other hand, the conquered people, 'inferiority' being 'the badge of all their tribe,' will display the vice of insincerity and, maybe, of prevarication, will become mere echoes of the opinions, or fancied opinions, of the over-ruling race, and, for want of scope and influence, be unable to find full play for their abilities, or employment for their experience. The most melancholy feature of the whole matter is that, by so acting, they rivet the chains of subjection more firmly upon themselves. ''Tis true, 'tis pity; pity 'tis, 'tis true.' Such is the state of things we have brought about in India. If, nevertheless, it is possible for one to give such a favourable account of the Indian people as appears in the foregoing pages, evidence is furnished of the

Self-praise of Indian administration.

great possibilities of the race, if placed under more favourable circumstances. We praise ourselves in season, and out of season, for what we have done in India, and for the way in which we have done it; we depreciate our Indian fellow-subjects in equal ratio. But, as we are judging our own work, and as our estimate of the Indians is the estimate of an over-lording class, our praise of ourselves and our depreciation of others must be accepted with caution. We have been in India many years. We have failed to govern the country as *Failure to properly govern India.* it ought to be governed, not so much from want of good intentions as from deficiency of knowledge, and, what is far worse, we are rendering it impossible for the people ever to rule themselves. What we, because of our shallow information, have not succeeded in doing ourselves, we will not admit to be possible of accomplishment by those who possess the knowledge and experience which we lack. It may be denied that our rule in India has been a practical failure. To such deniers there is a three-fold answer. That answer is wholly made up of facts furnished by those who are responsible for what is described. It cannot truthfully be asserted that our rule has been a success, when,

I.—*Forty millions of people are in a chronic state of* *Forty millions starving.* *starvation.*

II.—*During the past twenty years over nine millions of* *Nine millions died from want of food.* *people have died from want of food.*

III.—*In twenty years, i.e., during the period between* 1858 *Great increase of public debt.* *and* 1879, *India has been under the direct rule of Great Britain, we have trebled the public debt, raising it from between fifty and sixty millions to between one hundred and forty and one hundred and fifty millions.*

So far as the mass of the inhabitants are concerned, *British rule worse than native in time of calamity.* all this time—as I have already shown, and shall show in fresh detail—life has been made increasingly hard to them : their struggle for existence has become fiercer, their life far less worth living. It has happened that precisely in accord with the prevalence of the more complete English mode of rule (save and except, under Lord Northbrook, in Behar, in 1874) in time of calamity, the suffering of the people has been greatest : where native administration has had sway the conditions have been easier and better for the sufferers. This *Native administration in famine times.* was strikingly manifested during the famine of 1876-1877. Mysore and the Nizam's Dominions are both Native States. The first-named State, at that time, was under the special con-

trol of the Government of India, and was administered by a
strong force of English officials. To say nothing of the
money-loss involved in crop-failure, the destruction in other
respects was frightful; one fourth of the population was swept
away. In the latter State, where an able Indian statesman
holds the reins of power, the distress was grappled with in a
masterly manner in the earlier stages of the calamity, and the
death-rate was only slightly above the average. The Nizam's
Dominions had practically recovered from the famine within
a year or two of the height of the distress. It will take Mysore
a generation, or may be a century, to completely recover itself.
Comparison between Sir Salar Jung's districts, and those in the
Madras and Bombay Presidencies, again under British control,

Comparison favourable to native administration. exhibits the same features as would a comparison between the
two Native States. In the Nizam's Dominions you have the
English system of administration thoroughly grasped by an
Indian statesman, modified so much as might be necessary to
meet existing circumstances, and carried out by Indian agency.
The result is far superior to what can be accomplished where
English ideas are carried out by English officials, who are aliens
and foreigners—who do not thoroughly understand either
country or people, and, what is worse, in too many instances,
do not care to try to understand them. Herein lies the radical defect of our present arrangements in India, and until a
change is made, neither will India be so well-ruled as it ought
to be, nor will justice be done to the country, and its inhabitants.

Indian experience not sufficiently availed of. India is in a worse condition than it would have been had
our countrymen relied less upon their own theories, and trusted
more to the experience stored in native minds, which
experience was available to them, had they cared to seek it.
The fact need hardly be stated—it is so patent—that Indians,
while not unmindful of certain benefits which have accrued to
their country from British supremacy (indeed, the leaders of
Indian opinion are always ready to pay the sincerest homage to
such good as has been accomplished), would be reluctant to
admit that our rule, on the whole, has been all that could be

desired, or has made for the lasting good of the land. But, because their attitude towards us must be hostile, it does not at all follow that their opinions are valueless. On the contrary. And, it is noteworthy, the worst the Indians say about their country, and its decadence in some respects, is more than borne out by independent observers. For instance, the memorandum prepared and published by Mr. J. Caird, C.B., after his visit to India in connection with the Famine Commission is a serious indictment of the manner in which the country is administered. Special apologists, such as Mr. Justice Cunningham, of the High Court of Justice, Calcutta, and others, against their will and in spite of their denials, are compelled to support the views of outside observers. Mr. Cunningham has recently produced a work, 'British India and its Rulers.' Like Sir Richard Temple's 'India in 1880,' it is intended as a glorification of our rule. Yet the Judge is compelled to state that the old native manufactures have died out, or have been superseded by European fabrics. He also admits that famines have occurred with great regularity, and with terrible effect. Since the beginning of this century there have been eleven great famines, which have affected large provinces. Some part of India suffers from famine two years in every nine ; a famine of some sort or other may be expected every eleven or twelve years; and a great famine—such as that which devastated Madras in 1876-1877, or Bengal in 1774—may come twice in a century. *

Justice Cunningham's admissions.

The Prime Minister of the Maharajah Holkar, in a Memorandum on Famines in India, does not hesitate to assert that in his opinion, and in the opinion of those who, like him, have special and full knowledge, great decadence has accompanied our administration. ' In the fourteenth century,' says Mr. Raghunath Rao, ' there was only one famine in India. In the fifteenth century it was the same. In the seventeenth century there were two famines. In the

Indian opinion on increase of Famines.

---

* The *Saturday Review* is constrained to say of Mr. Justice Cunningham's optimism, " With all these averages and uncertainties, it seems idle to dilate on the happiness" of Indian proprietorship.

C

eighteenth there were eight famines. In seventy-seven years
of the nineteenth centuiy, there were more than twelve
famines ; I am told there have been eighteen famines.'
There may be unintentional exaggeration here, as local
severe scarcities, in the present century, are probably counted
as famines ; in past centuries they would, most likely, have
passed away unrecorded. The very able and exhaustive
report on the Famine in the Nizam's Dominions, prepared by
Maulvi Mahdi Ali, Revenue Secretary at Hyderabad, however,
gives evidence which goes entirely to support the position
taken by the Maharajah Holkar's Minister.

Taxation.

As regards taxation, Dr. Hunter, speaking from the
superficial view which it is scarcely pardonable in one with
so much information at his command, to take, asserts that the
taxation of to-day is very light and easily borne. Those who
carry the burden speak of it in a different manner. Absolute
contradiction of Dr. Hunter's statement is to be found in the
fact that the Government of India are at their wits' end to im-
Onerous na- pose an additional tax, and in the further fact that special
ture of Taxation legislative measures have been passed again and again in
relief of the taxpayers.* The continual grinding condition of

---

* An Indian newspaper which, for its readiness to do for the Government of India what
Balaam, the prophet, would not do for King Balak, viz., prophesy smooth things, simply
because smooth prophecies are wanted, has become a bye-word in India—I mean the *Pioneer*
—writing in 1877 of agrarian discontent in Bombay, was compelled to say, "Worried by the
revenue survey for heavily-enhanced public payments, enslaved by his private creditor,
dragged into Court only to have imposed upon him the intolerable burden of fresh decrees,
without even the resource of flight, which was open to his fore-fathers before the kindred
scourge of Holkar, the Deccan ryot accepted, for the third of a century, with characteristic
patience and silence, the yoke of British mis-government. For thirty years, as we now learn
from the papers published, he had been at once the scandal and anxiety of his masters.
Report upon report had been written upon him ; shelf upon shelf in the public offices
groaned under the story of his wrongs. If any one doubts the naked accuracy of these
words, let him dip into the pages of Appendix A (papers on the indebtedness of the
agricultural classes in Bombay). *A more damning indictment was never recorded against a
civilised Government.* From 1844 to 1874, successive Administrations have been appealed to,
have been warned, or have been urged. Each, in its turn, has replied—as the present will
doubtless answer to the late Committee's importunities—with a suave sigh of *non possumus.*
The hospitalities of Dapoore or Ganeshkhind (the palaces of the Bombay Governor) have for
thirty years been lavished in graceful and generous profusion ; while the ryot, who paid for
them, laid hard by in enforced and ruinous idleness, a debtor in the Poona gaol ; or ate at
their gates, in the field of which the fruits had once been his own, the bitter bread of
slavery." Commenting upon this passage, Mr. C. H. O Donnell, B.C.S., in his pamphlet,
"The Ruin of an Indian Province," says :—"It is true that this seems the language of
exaggeration ; yet, after making every allowance for the influence of a just indignation, it is
impossible to assert that the history of this century presents many more fearful pictures of
maladministration by a European nation than does this paragraph from one of the most
Conservative journals in the Empire." "So," continues the newspaper, "the survey officers
(of the land revenue) came and went, *adding each his thousands and tens of thousands to the*

poverty suffered by the ryot, and his utter helplessness in the hands of the money-lender, also contradict the optimistic remarks of officials. Let us see, however, what representative native opinion says on this point. Mr. Raghunath Rao writes :—'In the good old days one-sixth of the net produce was the share of the Sovereign.' The Ayeen Akbarry remarks :—'In former times the monarchs of Hindoostan exacted the sixth of the produce of the lands ; in the Turkish Empire the husbandman paid the fifth, in Taran the sixth, and in Iran, the tenth.' Noorshurvan, King of Persia, fixed it at a third. Akbar settled his land-tax at one-third of the medium produce. His unworthy successors raised it to one-half. *Now, in practice, it is considerably higher than one-half.* About the late famine in the Bombay Presidency, the opinion of the natives may be learnt from the following :— 'While the harvests were not good, the assessment on land was heavily enhanced. The peasantry were thus impoverished in two ways. In the first place, the out-turn of their crops was not favourable, and in the second, they were called upon to pay an enhanced land revenue demand. The famine of 1876 found the agricultural classes in this condition, and they

Ancient im-posts.

Native opinion on Bombay famine.

---

public assessments. Marwaris (money-lenders) swarmed up, in ever-increasing flights, from the far north-west, and settled down on the devoted acres. Honourable Justices visited India, to carry off after a while to their homes, also, some trifle from the ryot's hands, leaving him in exchange their precedents and their rulings ; leaving also, in a thousand desolate homesteads, a monument, to those who sought it, of the wisdom of the system over which (always, of course, at the ryot's expense) it had been their pleasure to preside. Decrees of the Courts flew like arrow-flights into the thickest of the population, striking down the tallest and the most notable. *Stupidity, blindness, indifference, greed—inability, in a word, in all its thousand forms—settled down, like the fabled harpies, on the ryot's bread, and bore off with them all that he subsisted upon.* Then, at last, in spite of his marvellous forbearance, Jacques Bonhomme could stand it no longer. Long-suffering in every land, the patience in India of the *misera contribuens plebs* is especially proverbial. Conversely, in India of all other countries, are agricultural movements dangerous." Mr. O'Donnell, in comment, says, "It may well be wonderingly asked, Can it be possible that the highly-civilised Government of England in the nineteenth century can have reduced a great Indian province to that worst extremity of peasant misery which has made the great French social war of the fourteenth century a bye-word for criminal maladministration? Truly and piteously did Sir George Wingate, a distinguished Bombay officer, exclaim : 'What must be the state of things which can compel cultivators, proverbially patient and long-suffering, accustomed to more or less of ill-usage and injustice at all times, to redress their wrongs by murder, and in defiance of an ignominious death to themselves? How must their sense of justice have been violated? How must they have been bereft of all hope of redress from law or Government before their patient and peaceful natures could be roused to the point of desperation required for such a deed?'" "It is difficult," adds the *Pioneer*, "to read these sentences without something like a curse on the system of *laisser aller* which drove the Kumbi from his fields to his only effective form of argument ; without something like fiery anger at the Government which has replied, once and for all, to his pleading, by thrusting him into a gaol."

could ill stand its pressure. The inevitable consequence has been widespread distress and considerable loss of human life.'

Unjust dealings with Ryots. In a foot-note, I have given a citation from Mr. O'Donnell's pamphlet of the wrong done to Bombay ryots. I may take over here some evidence which he supplies of the condition of the people in a Bengal province, viz., that of Behar, in which the famine of 1874 occurred. The *Englishman* newspaper, the oldest and most respected daily paper in Calcutta, records facts highly discreditable in regard *Running away from British rule.* to Behar. 'The absconding of ryots,' it writes, 'has become so notorious that the police have been employed to register their flight. During the year 1874-1875, in spite of splendid harvests, over five thousand families have sought refuge from English injustice in the jungles of the Nepaulese Terai. It is calculated that these five thousand households, thus abandoned, represent a total number of emigrants not less than twenty thousand.' These statements, says Mr. O'Donnell, far from being contradicted, were confirmed beyond question in every particular. A judicial officer of tried ability was deputed to inquire into the disorder, assisted by the chief magistrate of the Durbhunga district. ' Quite apart,' he wrote, ' from the failure of crop, in travelling there ' *Depopulation.* —the Durbhunga property—' one had a feeling sometimes of *desolateness,* from the fewness of the people to be met on the road, or to be seen on the maidans (plains). The villages were few. We were so much struck with the scantiness of population that, in the absence of people enough to ask about it, we began speculating to ourselves as to the cause why old fields should have been abandoned, why good wastes should not have been reclaimed. . . . . I have further to submit that the anxiety among the population of these estates, as I understood their feelings, was about impending ruin, rather than impending starvation. It is true, they talked of famine and death ; but this was, for the most part, but a prelude to *Invariable tale of oppression.* the *invariable tale of oppression and rack-renting.* I watched them carefully—their expression, their demeanour, the subjects up to which they led the conversation—and the above was the conclusion I came to.' Mr. O'Donnell, in his pamphlet, proceeds to give, from official records, facts which prove that the illegal exactions, rack-renting, and other misdoings, for which the authorities were responsible, did more to bring about and accentuate the sufferings caused by the famine of 1874 than all the mischances of climate, drought, or inundation.

The soil of the country, too, is proving less productive year by year, thereby adding to the aggravations of the situation. While the present state of things continues, while we deny to the people that share in their own government which would stimulate them to earnestness of effort, and to fertility of resource—because their interest in the prosperity of their own country, brought about by themselves, would be greater—little change can be hoped for. There is nothing, save the blighting influence of the stranger, to prevent the Indian soil from becoming very fertile. Japan and China are equally ancient in the scale of nations with India. The Japanese and the Chinese maintain the fertility of their soil. The influences which are potent with them would be likewise potent with the people of India if only they were assisted to help themselves, put in the way of self-advancement, and then largely left to their own devices.

Soil less productive.

Blighting influence of the stranger.

Japanese and Chinese cultivation good.

If, under our care, Indian agriculture has proved increasingly less productive, that is not the only ill done to India which can be laid to our charge. We have killed the manufactures of the country : even Mr. Justice Cunningham admits this. At one time the looms of India must have given much occupation to weavers. The needs of two hundred millions of people, at least, were met therefrom. Now, save and except in Madras, Bombay, and one or two other towns, where cotton-mills have been established by Indian mercantile energy, the occupation of weaving has become comparatively scarce, and almost worthless. I will not weary the reader with statistics on the point : they are at hand for the curious who may desire

Indian manufactures killed by British.

them. As an example of the harm which has been wrought, Mr. Mahdi Ali's answer to a question put to him by the Famine Commission in 1878 will suffice. ' In the Nizam's Dominions,' he said, 'the manufacturing classes have broken down in the same way as they have done in other parts of India. The famous brocades of Aurungabad, the silk stuffs turned out by the looms at Paitan, the filigree work of Bidar, the carpets of Warrangal, and the cotton stuffs of Nander, all these manufactures are on the wane, and these industries are fast dying out of the country.' It is we of the English race who have killed these industries. Upon us lies the serious responsibility of repairing the mischief we have done, and—let the efforts needed be never so toilsome—to take care that we leave, or—if some object to the expression of such a contingency—that we are careful to govern India better than we found it governed.

Evidence from the Deccan.

Finances. It is unnecessary that much should be said in this Letter respecting the Finances of India. No one at all acquainted with public affairs can be unaware of the grave position of the financial administration of the Empire. A few general remarks, however, may not be without value. Taking the figures of the past forty years, it appears that only in eleven years has the income sufficed to meet the expenditure and leave a surplus ; in twenty-nine years there have been deficits. For one year of solvency there have been two of insolvency. Sometimes, as in 1860, the deficit for the year has reached nearly fifteen millions, or as in 1861, over twelve millions, while the surplus at its highest (1866) has been only two-and-three-quarters of a million. The net deficit on the whole period under review was £76,908,484. Since 1840 the public debt has more than quadrupled : the interest paid upon it since 1840, viz., £148,323,967, is £2,488,527 more than the amount of the debt in 1879—the sum total then being £145,835,440. Other totals of importance show that, in the thirty-eight years under review, £687,275,726 were derived as taxation from Land, and £227,097,608 from the tax on Opium.

Frequent and heavy deficits.

Quadrupling of public debt.

The Opium traffic, the continuance of which is a sore burden upon the conscience of Great Britain, in 1840 yielded only three-quarters of a million. The year after it doubled in value. Now it amounts to nearly ten millions : the net receipts to the Treasury are between six and seven millions ; the remainder is swallowed up in establishments and the like. After our war with China, to compel that country to take Indian Opium, the traffic greatly increased. The reader will see that the crime which we have committed—for, in the Court of Righteousness, if not in the Law Courts of the Empire, we are held to have done iniquitously—is entirely committed within the memory of living men, and has—ignorantly or otherwise—been fostered by the existing generation of Englishmen. A striking act of political justice would be performed if the generation which witnessed the portentous up-growth of the traffic, which allowed the growth to go on unchecked, were to prove the generation which got rid of it altogether. Stoppage of the traffic is possible, without causing bankruptcy. A separate pamphlet, however, would be needed to show this ; that pamphlet must await the course of events.

In this connection an incident must not be over- looked which gives present and very pressing importance to the opium question. Chinese diplomacy is of an unusually patient and utterly tireless kind. Once let the ruling mind of China be set upon the accomplishment of an object, and, 'without haste, without rest,' that object will be accomplished. The recent conflict with Russia in connection with the Kuldja Treaty affords proof that the Chinese diplomatic grip is like the tooth-hold of an English bull-dog in battle : once fixed, then death or victory. The remarkable letter from his Excellency Li Hung Chang, to the Rev. F. Storrs Turner, Secretary of the Anti-Opium Society, followed up as it has been by the despatch of an unaccredited Envoy to Calcutta, to make enquiries in India, shows that China has determined to be rid of the Indian Opium traffic. At their own convenience, the Chinese authorities will press the matter for settlement, in a manner unpleasant for India. Whether a Radical or Tory Government were in power in Great Britain when that time arrived, it is certain that the awakened conscience of the nation would not permit another war of iniquity with the Celestials for the maintenance of a portion of the Indian revenue. Whether we like it or not, we shall one day be compelled to readjust our Indian finances so as to make both sides of the account balance without the contribution now forced from the Chinese. It is obvious that enlightened statesmanship should be directed towards bringing about the inevitable change at a time which would be convenient to Great Britain, and to India, and not be forced to take this action whenever it might suit China to make the demand.

Salt taxation. As taxes upon Salt—from 1840 to 1879—£157,120,787 were contributed by the Indian people. On the subject of the salt tax, and its collection, I may repeat a portion of a conversation I had, while residing in India, with an English Civil Servant of the Madras Presidency. 'You refer to the Salt Tax,' said this official. ' Well, for my part, I consider the law with reference to it is most iniquitous. I have recently been magistrate in the taluk of ——, and almost every day had to try a number of frauds on the salt revenue, as they are termed. It distressed me exceedingly to pass sentences upon the poor wretches brought before me, but my duty was to administer the law, and I took care to do it as humanely as possible. Here is an instance of the way in which the law works. A case came before me in which a labourer had shifted his place of residence, and had made himself a new mud hut. When he came to occupy his hut, he found the earth-floor strongly impregnated with saline particles ; he scraped up some of the dirt, separated the parts as well as he could, and put the "salt" he had collected outside to dry. This was observed by a revenue collector ; the man was proceeded against, was imprisoned, and was condemned to receive some lashes, but the last part Mr. Caird on onerous Salt of the sentence was remitted.' Mr. Caird, in his 'Notes of duties. an Indian Journey,' mentions a visit he made to a place in

Bengal, where he asked the price of salt, and found the tax upon it amounted to nine-tenths of the price. That is, in buying five-pennyworth of salt, one half-penny represents the value of the condiment, and fourpence-halfpenny the tax upon it.

The onerous character of the taxation we have imposed upon India may be judged, if we note the increase of the one item of revenue derivable from salt. The period we have under review is that already mentioned, viz., from 1840 to 1879, both years inclusive. During that time the population, allowing for checks by famine and by other calamities—(in one night, in the delta of the Megra river in Bengal, nearly one hundred thousand people were drowned by a cyclonic wave sweeping across the low level country)—the increase cannot have been more than, at the outside, twenty per cent. As a matter of fact, it has been less, but we will accept that estimate. While, however, the increase of population has been only twenty per cent. or less, *the increase in the receipts of the taxation on salt has been nearly three hundred per cent.* That is, salt is now several times dearer, owing entirely to higher taxation, than it was in 1840! Yet Englishmen are told, by official apologists, that we have made life easier and better for our Indian fellow-subjects, that all the advantages of our rule—and they, it is said, are legion—have been for the people. Rather, it seems that while the native rulers whipped the people with whips we have scourged them with scorpions. About eight years ago, Mr. J. H. Keene, of the Bengal Civil Service, Judge at Agra, wrote a poem which appeared in all the Indian papers. In that poem, apostrophizing English supremacy, Mr. Keene asked,—

Onerous character of taxation.

Enormous increase in salt revenue.

' What has your civilization done for the people here ?
Has it made them prosper ?—or poorer ?—think you, year by year ?
Skulking in rotten cabins, like foul and famished ghosts ;
While you live at Simla concocting statistics and well-paid posts ;
Standing like trees between the soil and the beams of God,
Furnishing each clod-hopper with one supporting clod ?
This is not your ideal ? Well, and what is it then ?
Flatulent Bengal students aping the manners of men ?
People that hate you like poison, praising you up to the skies,
Greeks of the lower Empire building a throne on lies ? '

Crushing weight of ad-
ministration.

When, side by side with the increased cost of salt, an absolute necessity of healthy life, we put the greater cost of food-grains of all kinds (see *ante*, p. 13), some idea may be formed of the terribly crushing weight of English administration upon the inhabitants of India. It would be tedious here to follow out the several acts of our statesmen which have led to so discreditable an issue. A glance at the revenue returns confirms the opinion formed on the spot in India, as to the unsatisfactory nature of our rule. After seeing with one's own eyes what is to be seen, the conclusion cannot be avoided that nearly the whole course of present trouble arises from the fearful and unnecessary expense of our way of doing things in a country which we won by craft and by the sword, and which we are only able to keep by deeds of oppression and by resources wrung from the vitals of the people. It is time to put an end to this state of things, or—if things have progressed so far that an end is not possible, except at the cost of more effort than even a resolute people like the British would be prepared to undertake—that there was such an immediate grappling with the subject as shall, at least, procure amelioration. Now that India is virtually ruled by the House of Commons, every Englishman is guilty of serious dereliction of duty who does not strive, so far as in him lies, first, to understand the country and the people, and, then, steadily and unweariedly, to use every means in his power to bring relief to the suffering and oppressed.

III.—WHAT ENGLISHMEN CAN DO FOR INDIA.

I FEEL satisfied no really earnest Liberal, whose reason for existence as a Liberal is that he may right wrongs and redress grievances, can read the foregoing pages without experiencing a desire to know in what way he can exercise his influence on behalf of fellow-subjects who seem so greatly to need help of some kind or other. Since my return from India, scarcely anything in the conduct of my countrymen has struck me more than their pathetic wish to uplift India, their strenuous desire to do something for the Indian people, if only they knew how to act, if they could only learn what there is for them to do. The first requisite is to understand the people to whom we desire to give our friendliest help. Before everything else the Englishman's mind must be cleared of cant about the inferiority of the Indian and his excessively wicked character. I trust the earlier pages of this Letter will be useful in helping some, at least, of my countrymen to believe better things, to form a higher estimate, of the Queen's lieges in India than they have hitherto been accustomed to do, not from want of will, I am quite sure, but from want of knowledge, or from their being the victims of prejudice. The view of the Indian people, which I have given, is not the fashionable one : I know it is the true one so far as my own personal observation is concerned, and so far as I have been able to test *experience* in others. I also know that it is only in the adoption by British electors of such a view as I have indicated, and by action appropriate taken thereupon, the regeneration of India may come. Then it may come, whence alone it can come, viz., from the sons of the soil. Only by remedial effect of this kind it is possible for us to cleanse out souls, in however slight a degree, of the wrong we have done in the past. The way before us, to a better state of things, may be long, the difficulties in the path leonine : nevertheless there lies our duty. I am persuaded, if my fellow-countrymen could but appreciate things as they are in India, sooner or later, and sooner rather than later, the right course would be taken.

The misconceptions which have to be cleared from our minds before we can hope to understand the needs of India do not apply to individuals merely : they affect the whole range of efforts commonly current relating to the country. Englishmen, as a rule, are not made acquainted with India as it is. Their conceptions generally are formed upon impressions gained from official utterances, the prevailing Roseate utter- tone of which is always roseate. That is, to the hasty glance. It is only by close research, and reading between the lines, that official documents, in many instances, are found to contain most damaging statements regarding our rule. On the face of things, all is smooth and satisfactory : the balance sheet for the year seems satisfactory. It is only afterwards that the accounts are found to be eight millions wrong, that this sum had actually been spent, when the accounts are made up, and no record of the expenditure appeared. Not wishing for a moment to impute to anyone a conscious desire to mislead, I cannot refrain from saying that a more complete misunderstanding is not possible than is contained in the ideas which may be formed upon the statements of those who, from the official standpoint, address the English public on Indian affairs. Dr. Hunter, the Editor of the *Imperial Gazetteer* of India, during his residence in Britain, has delivered lectures in Birmingham and elsewhere, on what England has done for India. In those lectures there is probably not a single assertion which, in itself, is not absolutely accurate, yet the whole Misleading in- effect of the deliverance is sadly misleading. India, as it is formation. known to those who have lived in the country, is hardly recognizable in Dr. Hunter's graphic descriptions. Still, even he, with all his predilections towards magnifying the good

Marginal notes:
Roseate utterances on India.
Misleading information.

and minimizing the bad of English rule, is unable to prevent Dr. Hunter the hideous truth in much of its painful nakedness occasionally becoming visible. The awful fact which I have put in the forefront in this Letter, viz., that forty millions of people are being continually on the verge of starvation, comes out, in Dr. Hunter's addresses, with reluctance, and as if against his will. Another example of the kind, but more glaringly unfair, is to be found in the handsome volume on 'India in 1880,' by Sir Richard Temple. Here, again, the facts cited, with one or two minor exceptions, cannot be gainsaid, but the total effect is inevitably to create a false impression. The 'India' of Sir Richard Temple is steeped in rose-colour, and Sir Richard Temple. is redolent with sweet perfumes. It is as correct a description of India in its varied moods as would be the exhibition of a picture—say, one of Sir Richard's own painting, which, in Indian galleries, have brought him no little praise— depicting the bewitching beauty of the morning dawn or evening twilight under tropical skies, which should be declared to be thoroughly satisfactory of all the moods, fierce noon-tide heat, terrible drought, awful cyclone, which the climate of India exhibits. Even the ghastly horrors of famine, and the maintenance of starving labourers on one pound weight of grain per day, in Sir Richard Temple's hands, become pleasant to the eye and endurable to the mind. India, although it has provided both fame and fortune to Sir Richard Temple and Dr. Hunter, ought not to be entrusted to them for exhibition—that is, if satisfaction is to be given either to Indians or to Britons, or, what is of greater importance, if violence is not to be done to truth.

The effect of such misleading presentations of Indian Effect of misleading information. affairs is to cause English public men to go sadly astray when, animated by the best intentions, they want to understand India. Nothing has more absolutely shown the necessity for accurate information than an article published some time ago in the *Nineteenth Century*, written by a scientific and popular Baronet, Member of Parliament for a learned constituency, whose general information is, as a rule, of a most precise and definite character. The Anglo-Indian Reformer sighs as he reads the Baronet's mistakes, and feels that if such a man goes wrong there is little hope of the average politician being right. So long as the statements of those whose interest it is to say peace where there is no peace (though they may not recognise the fact, and speak and write in good faith) are relied upon, correct ideas of India are impossible. The contention of the writer in the Review was that India had no cause of complaint against Great Britain, as she was not made to contribute anything to this country. In a direct form, it is true, no tribute is paid ; indirectly, however, England is draining India, not simply of its surplus, but actually of its very life-blood. Shortly before the close of the last session of Parliament, the Marquis of Hartington, Secretary of State for India, in answer to a question, admitted that nearly three millions sterling per annum are paid from the revenues of India to persons not resident in that country, as pensions and furlough pay.* The people of India, who possess full knowledge of the facts, do not agree with the honourable Baronet that England makes no profit out of her Indian connection. The Hon. Kristo Das Pal, Bahadur, C.I.E., in a speech which he made at a public meeting in Calcutta, puts matters in a light very different from that which shines, as through a glass darkly, from the pages of the English Review. The writer in the Review said, 'So far as military expenditure is concerned, the greatest care is taken that India should pay nothing beyond what is necessary for the troops actually on duty there. It is amusing, if so serious a subject can be amusing, to see how energetically the India Office resists any application made by the War Office for any charge beyond what the Indian authorities regard as absolutely necessary.' So much for theory. Now for facts. Said Mr. Kristo Das Pal, 'The War Office declares that a certain sum is needed ; that sum must be paid. The India

Marginal notes: England draining India.   Military expenditure.

---

* Lord Hartington's reply, furnished to him by the India Office, contained a serious inaccuracy, which may be found fully explained on page 487 of the *Statesman* (332, Strand, W.C.), for August.

Office and the Government of India could not interfere in the matter. England supplies the troops, and India is bound to pay whatever the conscience of the War Office demands. Then, it had been said that the principle on which the military charges were apportioned between England and India was one of joint partnership. Now, could a joint partnership exist between a giant and a dwarf? England was rich; India was poor. England governed herself through her House of Representatives; India was scarcely able to send forth her voice across a distance of ten thousand miles. Here and there, indeed, there were a few Englishmen—disinterested, philanthropic, warm-hearted Englishmen—who took an interest in the affairs of this country, but that was all. And yet they were told that the adjustment of military expenditure was conducted on the principle of joint partnership. If they examined the practical working of this joint partnership, what would they find? That on no less than seven occasions troops were borrowed from India—first, for the China expedition; next, for the Crimean war; thirdly, for the Persian expedition; fourthly, for the second China expedition; fifthly, for the first New Zealand expedition; sixthly, for the second New Zealand expedition; and, seventhly, for the Abyssinian war. All these were Imperial undertakings, but India had to furnish the troops with their pay and allowances. England, in fact, borrowed, and India paid. On the other hand, reinforcements were sent from England to India for the Sutlej campaign of 1846, the Panjab campaign of 1849, and for the mutiny campaign of 1857. How did India meet her liabilities in these cases? She had to pay every fraction of the pay of the troops from the moment they left England.' This is but one of a host of instances I might cite, save for the fear of becoming wearisome. It may be easily imagined how depressing such mistakes as those exposed above are to Indian Reformers, who desire that Englishmen should be correctly informed on the affairs of our great Indian Empire; and who desire that the

English and Indian partnership unequal.

India made to pay for English wars.

medium through which those affairs are regarded should be colourless.

English newspapers can go hopelessly wrong in regard to Indian facts, as well as English statesmen. During the period of the last Madras Famine, a weekly metropolitan journal, whose voice, on all political matters Indian, is always heard on the right side, made some unfortunate blunders when dealing with irrigation. In an article written on the failure of the monsoon rains, and the means which should be adopted to minimise the evil, the writer gravely proposed to meet the dearth of water by sinking an artesian well in each taluk, adding that this 'would reduce the losses of a famine year, at least by one-half, by rendering it possible to keep the animals alive.' Now, when it is remembered that the average size of a taluk in the Madras Presidency is seven hundred square miles, it will be pretty clear that the cattle at the outskirts will have to travel far for their morning and evening draught, to say nothing of the miraculous nature of the well intended to support so large an area. Probably, when taluk was written, village was meant. But in the same article appeared the following passage :—' We believe that the native form of irrigation, the formation of vast tanks, lakes, and reservoirs of water, *the method which made Tanjore a garden*, could be pursued to a much greater extent, without inordinate expense.' The writer ignores the Cauvery delta, and attributes the fertility of Tanjore to lakes, tanks, and reservoirs, the fact being that *there is not, in the whole delta, a single tank, lake, or reservoir used for irrigation*. There are, of course, small tanks in abundance used for bathing or drinking, or for cattle, but irrigation tanks there are none. There is a portion of the district, outside the limits of the delta, in which there may possibly be some irrigation tanks, but that region depends for its water supply on local rains, and is no better off in a deficient monsoon than the surrounding famine districts. It is the delta alone that deserves the name of a garden. It is constantly assumed by English writers that what has been done in Tanjore might be repeated in every district of the Presidency. But this

Marginal notes:
English journals at fault.
A well in each taluk.
Mistakes regarding irrigation.

supposition proceeds on complete ignorance of the climatic
conditions of the country.   The monsoon never fails altogether
on the West Coast, and rivers that take their rise there may *Irrigation limited by natural causes.*
always be depended upon.   There are, of course, differences
from year to year, but a few inches below the average make
little difference where the normal quantity is so large.   The
minimum rainfall on the West Coast seldom approaches what
can be called a failure of the monsoon.   The crops in Tanjore
scarcely ever fail, because the water supply comes largely
from the West Coast.   Similar conditions to those that have
created the fertility of Tanjore are found, to some extent, in
the deltas of the Kistna and the Godavari rivers, but they are
not found anywhere else in the Madras Presidency on a large
scale.   It ought not to be possible for mistakes of the character
I have just mentioned to be made.

The end which I, for one, have in view, viz., that the people *English help essential to Indian reform.*
of India may obtain a large share in the administration of
their own country, can be attained if only a determination
that it shall is come to by Englishmen.   India is now con-
trolled by the House of Commons.   Whatever the House
decides is done, no matter how disagreeable the decision may
be to particular individuals, who would fain resist the will
of the British people.   To the remark which may be made,
that to grant political power to the Indian people is to begin
their regeneration at the wrong end, that we must wait
for many years, and educate and train them still farther
before we do anything of the kind suggested, the answer is
easy.   Our own country, and all the other countries on the
globe which possess freedom, have shown that it is precisely *National advancement dependent upon popular freedom.*
in the same proportion as the mass of the population have some
share in the government of their country that great evils are
removed, that great advances are made.   It was only *after*
the Reform Bill of 1832, and the people properly so-called
exercised influence on the Legislature, that the progress we
are now so proud of was possible.   Freedom of trade, the
repeal of the Navigation Laws, National Education, Land
Law Reform in Ireland, have all followed from the broadening

D

of the base of power. Results of a like character would become apparent in India, if, with cautious wisdom, a similar course were pursued. Indeed, it is only as the scope for the exhibition of enterprise is provided for a nation that the enterprise can be displayed. Sir Thomas Munro, probably, the best Presi-dency Governor India has known, more than fifty years ago, uttered wise words, which ought now to be acted upon : ' There can be no hope,' he wrote, ' of any great zeal for improvement when the highest acquirements can lead to nothing beyond some petty office, and can confer neither wealth nor honour. While the prospects of the natives are so bounded, every project for bettering their character must fail, and no such projects can have the smallest chances of success, unless some of these objects are placed within their reach, for the sake of which men are urged to exertion in other countries. This work of improvement, in whatever way it may be accepted, must be very slow, but it will be in proportion to the degree of confidence we repose in them, and to the share which we give them in the administration of public affairs.' Such slight changes as have been made since Sir Thomas Munro's time have more than justified his predictions. India has within her borders,—the careers of such men as Sir Salar Jung, Sir Madhava Rao, Sir Dinkur Rao, Mr. Seshiah Sastri, the Hon. Kristo Das Pal, and a host of others, bearing testimony in what they have done,—sons capable of meeting the grave financial and social perils of the Empire, if only it be made possible for them to work their way to the front.

In India itself scarcely anything can be done in this direction. It is not easy, in a free country, to understand the obstacles to resolute forward action in India. A significant instance of what I mean occurred between four and five years ago. Because certain private gentlemen, impressed with a sense of the awful condition of the famine-stricken people around them, held a public meeting, and appealed to England for assistance, and did not, before so acting, obtain the consent of the Government of India, then in dignified seclusion at Simla, strenuous attempts were made to discredit their appeal.

Sir T. Munro on Indian advance.

Sir T. Munro's predictions justified.

Obstacles to forward action in India.

Only the resoluteness of the Relief Committee—resoluteness amounting almost to defiance of the Viceroy's authority—procured a reversal of the Governmental action. This reversal was signified by the transmission from the Viceroy, in the name of the Governor of Madras, to the Lord Mayor of London, of a telegram, stating that a misunderstanding prevailed : his Excellency, it was stated, really blessed the movement he was supposed to have banned. As a matter of fact his Excellency did bless the fund, for he gave ten thousand rupees to it and took a lively interest in the expenditure. But if the first ideas at Simla had prevailed, no fund would have been possible. In Calcutta, the Chief Justice of Bengal convened a meeting to collect subscriptions to send to Madras : pressure from Simla was applied there as it had been applied in Madras. Unfortunately, it was successful in Bengal, and for a time the founts of benevolence in Calcutta were partially dried up at a touch from the viceregal hand. This, which is a sample of what too often goes on in India when public opinion shows signs of movement, will serve to enforce what I have already said many times, viz., that effort on behalf of Indian reform which is to be of any service must proceed from the outside ; afterwards, local energy may be developed.

[margin note: Non-official defiance of the Viceroy.]

What, it appears to me, can be done, without any loss of time, is this : The National Liberal Federation might inscribe ' Justice for India ' on its banner, and appoint a Select Committee, whose duty it should be—

[margin note: Possible action in England.]

[margin note: Select Committee of Federation.]

1.—To watch the course of events in India and in England relating in any way to India ;

2.—To enter into communication with all known Indian Reformers and Reform Associations in this country and in the Empire, with a view of concentrating English and Indian opinion upon useful projects ;

3.—When occasion arises, the Executive Committee should be summoned, a statement of the circumstances necessitating the call made, and the advisability of communicating with all the branches of the Federation considered ; and

[margin note: Duties of a Select Committee.]

4.—If it be decided that it would be well to move in relation to the particular matter under notice, then a draft resolution should be sent to all the branches, accompanied by a collection of facts, specially prepared, for discussion : the resolution passed thereupon to be forwarded to Parliament or to the Secretary of State for India, accordingly as Parliament was or was not sitting at the time.

Instructed and well-informed opinion. By the adoption of some such means as these, a body of instructed and well-informed public opinion could be brought to bear at any moment that seemed desirable in the interests of the Empire. A double good would be effected. Our countrymen, in an attempt to help their fellow-subjects in India, would acquire a knowledge of that portion of the British Dominions which would be of the greatest benefit to them. Such an organization in this country would, through the recognised Associations in India—for example, the British Indian Association at Calcutta, the Sarvajanik Sabha in Poona, and others—be the means of throwing a flood of light upon matters now obscure. This is a duty which, I cannot but suppose, the members of the Federation will be proud to be instrumental in doing.

Broad lines of action. There are broad lines of action which may be decided upon at once, without waiting for special organization or for definite information from or about India. Mr. Bright's speech at the Mansion House, London, early in August, has made it quite clear that the Government will spend a portion of the recess in considering the means which should be taken Business arrangements in Parliament. to relieve the House of Commons from its present congested condition. It is impossible, of course, for anyone not in the secrets of the Cabinet to say what means will be adapted to this end. But it is conceivable that the idea of Grand Grand Committees. Committees for the discussion and arrangement of special departments of business will be considered. Upon that point, no doubt, the Federation, in its autumnal campaign, will have much to urge, in the way of suggestions, upon the Government. What I would beg is, that one of the points specially taken up should be this,—that an Indian Committee, consisting either wholly of Members of the House of Commons, or partly of Commons and partly of Peers, should be constituted : to them all proceedings relating to India, of whatever kind, should be submitted. Mr. Robert Knight, whose knowledge of the Empire is very great, in a Memorandum on India, which he has recently written, suggests that the Secretary of State for India should be a permanent official, and that a Committee of Members of the Houses of Peers and Commons six in number, should be associated with the Indian Secretary. For many reasons I think such a Committee would be too small ; I do not see, either, why members of the hereditary branch of the Legislature should be equal in number with the elected representatives of the country. What is wanted, above all things, in such a Committee is the fresh and healthy political feeling derivable only from the constituencies. Mr. Knight also urges the appointment of a Permanent Committee, which, again, I think a mistake. Let the members be eligible for re-election, but do not let them be irremovable. However, these are mere matters of detail. The great thing is the principle of having all Indian affairs brought prominently and regularly before this country.* Towards securing such an object, the Association I am addressing could exercise most powerful influence.

---

* In his Memorandum, Mr. Knight makes the following remarks, concerning a Permanent Committee :—It might be wise to appoint a Permanent Parliamentary Committee, to which all proceedings whatever of the India Office were submitted without reserve. Were such a Committee chosen from the few men in the two Houses who really know India, and were the proceedings of the India Office regularly submitted to their inspection, they would constitute an efficient "audit" of Indian affairs. They should have power to call for the most confidential, the most secret, documents ; and it would be their duty to bring before Parliament, and openly oppose therein, proceedings which they did not approve. They should have no power to do more than "report" to Parliament, and to lay bare before it the true character of our proceedings, that the nation might not be deceived and misled, as it now is, at all points concerning India. Such a Committee would be the "eye" of Parliament over all that was being done by the Indian Government. In the course of a very few years, the members who had been on this Permanent Committee would know all that it is essential for Parliament to know concerning the details of our administration. The occasions would not be numerous when they would find it necessary to "report" at all ; while their support of the Secretary for India in Parliament itself would be a guarantee of the propriety and wisdom of his proceedings, as the Committee should, of course, be selected without regard to Party.

And this great change in the character of the Secretaryship should be attended by a change of equal moment in the Indian Council. As now constituted, that Council is powerless for any good purpose. It has degenerated into a sort of outwork for defending the existing order of things in India, and for arresting all reform in our rule of that country. While the Council as now constituted is maintained, it will simply obstruct every reform that does not recommend itself to the conventional views and prejudices of its civilian

In relation to the Legislative Councils which exist in India, a great work has to be done which, I feel convinced, the Federation could accomplish. Some people, who know that India is ruled despotically, may be surprised to learn that there *are* Legislative Councils in the Empire. The Councils, however, are merely rudimentary institutions. No regular session is arranged for. The members are called together when the Governor-General, Governor, or Lieutenant-Governor thinks well to summon them. Each Presidency and Province has its Council. It consists generally of from twelve to fifteen members, Government officials forming a large majority. The ruler of the Empire, Presidency, or Province, presides over the Council, and by virtue of the power he possesses, and the influence he exerts, practically prevents even such plain-spoken observations as the rules would permit. The non-official members are selected by the Governor, one for each race in the Presidency or Province. The duties of the members are strictly confined to a consideration of new laws; these laws are submitted by the Government. The non-official members have no power of initiation. They are not allowed to ask any questions—either political, financial, social, or of any kind whatsoever. The Presidency or Provincial Budget is never so much as mentioned in the Council. A more anomalous position than that of these Councillors can scarcely be conceived : the

members. It should be done away with. It has become something very unpleasantly like a device for increasing the retiring allowances of men who have all their lives drawn immense allowances in India and amassed fortunes in that country, and to whom it is intensely pleasant to have their pension of £1,000 a year augmented by another £1,200 at the cost of the people of India, upon the pretext that they are earning this extra allowance by still devoting themselves to the service of that country. The English official members of the Council are allowed no such right, but draw only their Council allowances. Is it too much to expect that men who, upon the strength of their twenty-five years' service in India, are in receipt of very handsome pensions from its people, should on their retirement become an honorary Council for Her Majesty's Secretary of State? There is something degradingly selfish in our every arrangement concerning India. It is thought to be a great honour for Her Majesty to appoint the most distinguished of our public men at home to her Privy Council, without pay of any kind for the service required of them. Why should it be necessary to pay Her Majesty's Council of India, already handsomely provided for by the State, an extra salary of £1,200 a year simply for advising Her Majesty's Secretary of State an hour or two a week upon the conduct of its affairs? Let the Secretary of State be permanent, and let the Indian Council be an honorary body composed of retired Indians of all classes, with a reputation for ability and high character, whether they are official or non-official. Any distinguished Indian judge, lawyer, or merchant should be eligible thereto. Native gentlemen and native princes might also be invited to sojourn in England, by the serious compliment of asking them to come here to advise Her Majesty what she must do for India to rule it wisely and well. The Council of India should be a kind of Privy Council which Her Majesty's Secretary of State could summon, to advise with him in emergencies which must arise in a rule so strange as that of the Indian Empire.

amount of good they are able to effect is of the most in-appreciable kind. If English attention were directed towards a reform of these institutions, a beginning would be made which would constitute all other changes and developments possible : without reform of these Councils nine-tenths of any exertion put forth would be wasted. About four-and-a-half years ago, while editing a daily newspaper in Madras, I strongly advocated the establishment of Representative Assemblies, sketching in outline such a Chamber as that Presidency is, not merely fit for, but urgently needs to quicken the rich but stagnant mental life of the Madrasses of all classes and creeds. And, what is true of Madras is true also of Bengal and other parts of the Empire. Less than ten years ago, when speaking at Dacca, Sir George Campbell, M.P., then Lieutenant-Governor of Bengal, said that he looked forward to a time when a Bengali House of Commons would be created. The chief points of the scheme I put forward, while in India, were as follow :—

Reformed Councils, the first requisite.

Sir G. Campbell, M.P., on a Bengali House of Commons.

I.—The creation of a Presidency Assembly, in which the members of the Executive Council, H.E. the Governor excepted, should have seats *ex officio ;* also the Advocate General. In this Assembly, in addition, should sit (*a*) twenty Collectors (chief administrators of districts larger than many English counties) ; (*b*) six European, Eurasian and Native nominated members ; and (*c*) twelve European, Eurasian, and Native elected members. Qualification for a vote might be found in the jury lists, proved ownership of landed property, or payment of the profession tax. (An Assembly so constituted would leave the Government what, under existing circumstances, they should have, viz., a clear majority on any matter which might arouse much discussion and occasion great interest, or in relation to a measure which they felt the interests of the country demanded should be

A Presidency Assembly : its constitution.

carried, even though the majority of tne Assembly thought otherwise.)

Financial control.

2.—To such an Assembly *Financial control* should be given to this extent, viz., with the exception of Fixed Establishments, which should be discussed only with the consent of the Secretary of State first asked for and obtained, every vote of money should be open to scrutiny and question ; and (if permission had previously been given to Government Members to vote as they thought fit), on a 'majority being recorded against any particular vote, it could not be passed.

Right of questioning.

3.—Non-official members to have the right to put questions to Government on their general policy, or on a public matter.

Introduction of Bills.

4.—Non-official members to have the right to introduce Bills not dealing with public funds.

Budget to be annually presented.

5.—The Budget to be annually presented, and debated upon. No money to be spent until the same had been voted, Fixed Establishments excepted.

Fixed time of meeting.

6.—The Assembly to meet at certain fixed periods of the year.

Governor-General's Veto.

7.—The Governor-General to have the power to veto any Bill or Money Vote, subject to appeal to the Secretary of State for India, or the Home Government.

Subsidiary States be represented.

8.—Under certain defined arrangements, subsidiary States, such as Travancore, Cochin, &c., to be permitted to send representatives to the Assembly.

Suggestions approven by—

There was not a class in the community which did not hail these suggestions with heartiness. English merchants, true to their national character, were strongly in favour of some

(1) Anglo-Indians.

such change as was indicated. To men, nurtured in the free air of England, life in the despotically-ruled cities of India, is

(2) Natives.

like breathing in a partially exhausted air-receiver. The intelligent Hindus and Mussalmans of Madras, seeing the increased importance and power such an Assembly would give to their national existence, and recognizing the scope it would afford for individual usefulness, gave the suggestions their hearty approval. Even Members of the Civil Service approved it. (3) Civil servants. One of the Executive Councillors declared that Southern (4) Executive Councillors. India was quite ripe for such an Assembly, and that untold good would follow from its establishment. Nevertheless, the agitation I sought to initiate, came to nothing. It made a slight Agitation failed—reason why. ripple on the surface of everyday talk, and then passed away. Nor do I wonder that such was the case, although I deeply regretted at the time the apathy exhibited, and the many obstacles in the way of attracting attention to the matter. Afterwards the famine of 1877 diverted all attention from schemes of reform for a time. I see now more forcibly than I did then the utter futility of agitation in India alone ; unless there be simultaneous agitation to the same end in England no good can be done. Previously, in Ceylon, when condemning the food-taxes and revenue-farming system in that island, I found that until I had enlisted the help of the Cobden Club, and the services in Parliament of Mr. T. B. Potter, M.P. for Rochdale, I was nearly helpless. With these aids the task of attracting attention to serious evils became comparatively easy of accomplishment.

In advocating the reform of the Legislative Councils of Legislative Council Reform safe. India, Englishmen would be on perfectly safe ground. By no possibility could the charge of want of information, if brought by interested opponents, be honestly employed against the Federation. But, what is of far greater importance, the establishment of such Assemblies would lead the way to, and prepare the people for, that change in the administration of India which must come some day ; until it does come little hope for real *Indian* rule can be cherished.

The remark I have just made has no relation to the Mr. Bright's proposals in 1853. giving up of India, but to the proposal made by Mr. Bright, in 1858, when the India Bill was under consideration in the House of Commons, viz., that the country should be divided

Five or six
Presidencies. into five or six Presidencies or Provinces, each under a
separate Governor, who should be in direct communication
with the Secretary of State. In each Presidency there should
be an Assembly. It has been Mr. Bright's good fortune, as
a statesman, to find that most of the advance posts he occupied
by virtue of his prescient mind at the beginning of his political
career have formed camping grounds for the main army of progress. His proposal with regard to India will, I believe, yet
rank with his fulfilled prophecies on such subjects as Free
Trade, Parliamentary Reform, Abolition of Church Rates,
Land Law Reform, and other matters. All that I have seen
of India, all that I have learned of its peoples and their needs,
all that I have thought upon urgent changes, compel me to
Mr. Bright's the conclusion that to work for Mr. Bright's ideal is to work
ideal practicable
and necessary. for a reform not merely practicable but highly necessary;
and also, practically, to bring the Empire within a measurable
distance of thoroughly good and stable Government, wherein
the scandal of forty millions of people remaining in a state
of semi-starvation year after year shall be impossible. We
cannot hinder that condition of things by our action, as we
have proved : the people of India may prevent it by their own
efforts.

The passages from Mr. Bright's speech of June 24, 1858,
to which I have referred, may be cited at length. They meet, in
a satisfactory way, the initial objections which would be urged
by those opposed to such reforms on their re-presentation.
Mr. Bright said :—

Presidencies, 'I would propose that we should have Presidencies, and
not an Empire. not an Empire. If I were a minister, which the House will
admit is a bold figure of speech, and if the House were to
agree with me, which is also an essential point, I would
Five Presi- propose to have, at least, five Presidencies in India, and I
dencies : equal would have the Governments of those Presidencies perfectly
rank. equal in rank and in salary. The capitals of those Presidencies would probably be Calcutta, Madras, Bombay, Agra,
and ,Lahore. I will take the Presidency of Madras as an
illustration. Madras has a population of some 20,000,000.

We all know its position on the map, and that it has the advantage of being more compact, geographically speaking, than the other Presidencies.   It has a Governor and a Council. I would give to it a Governor and a Council still, but would confine all their duties to the Presidency of Madras, and I would treat it just as if Madras was the only portion of India connected with this country.   I would have its finance, its taxation, its justice, and its police departments, as well as its public works and military departments, precisely the same as if it were a State having no connection with any other part of India, and recognized only as a dependency of this country. I would propose that the Government of every Presidency should correspond with the Secretary for India in England,* and that there should be telegraphic communications between the office of the noble Lord (Lord Stanley) and every Presidency over which he presides.   I shall, no doubt, be told that there are insuperable difficulties in the way of such an arrangement, and I shall be sure to hear of the military difficulty. Now, I do not profess to be an authority on military affairs, but I know that military men often make great mistakes.   I would have the army divided, each Presidency having its own army, just as now, care being taken to have them kept distinct ; and I see no danger of any confusion or misunderstanding, when an emergency arose, in having them all brought together to carry out the views of the Government.

'Now, suppose the Governor-General gave the Presidencies established, the Governors equal in rank and dignity, and their Councils constituted in the manner I have indicated, is it not reasonable to suppose that the delay which has hitherto been one of the greatest curses of your Indian Government would be almost altogether avoided ?   Instead of a Governor-General living in Calcutta or at Simla, never

Each Presidency self-contained.

Government to correspond with Secretary of State.

Military difficulty considered

Advantages of separate Presidencies.

Delays avoided

---

* Direct correspondence with the Secretary of State is a privilege which the Presidency of Madras retains as a survival of old times.   Good use of this privilege was made in 1878 by the (then) Governor of Madras, who, when compelled by the Government of India to adopt Sir Richard Temple's 1-lb. starvation allowance for famine labourers, appealed to England, and procured permission to set aside superior orders.   The wisdom of Mr. Bright's suggestion was then strikingly manifested.   Many thousands of lives were saved by the direct appeal to England.—W. D.

travelling over the whole of the country, and knowing very little about it, and that little only through other official eyes, is it not

Governmental action more direct. reasonable to suppose that the action of the Government would be more direct in all its duties, and in every department of its service, than has been the case under the system which has existed until now ? Your administration of the law, marked

Law administra-tion improved. by so much disgrace, could never have lasted so long as it has done, if the Governors of your Presidencies had been indepen-dent Governors. So with regard to matters of police, education,

Presidencies rivals in good works. public-works, and everything that can stimulate industry, and so with regard to your system of taxation. You would have in every Presidency a constant rivalry for good. The Governor of Madras, when his term of office expired, would be delighted to show that the people of that Presidency were contented, that the whole Presidency was advancing in civilization, that roads and all manner of useful public works were extending, that industry was becoming more and more a habit of the people, and that the exports and imports were constantly increasing. The Governors of Bombay and the rest of the Presidencies would be animated by the same spirit, and so you would have all over India, as I have said, a rivalry for good ; you would have placed a check in that malignant spirit of

Incidental ad-vantages. ambition which has worked so much evil, you would have no Governor so great that you could not control him ; none who might make war when he pleased ; war and annexation would be greatly checked, if not entirely prevented ; and I do, in my conscience, believe you would have laid the foundation for a better and more permanent form of Government for India than has ever obtained since it came under the rule of Eng-land.' *

Mr. Bright's ideas practical. To the eye of an observer, unacquainted, by residence in India, with the actual necessities of that country, Mr. Bright's remarks must carry conviction. I have only to add that to one who knows India they seem to meet the situation with perfect nicety. I will not go into particulars, showing the

---

* Speeches by the Right Hon. John Bright, M.P. Edited by J. Thorold Rogers, M.P. Vol. I., pp. 50-53. (Macmillan & Co., London, 1869.) Second Edition.

differences between the various portions of the Empire which *Needs of the Empire render change needful.* render it advisable that each Presidency should have its own almost independent administration. Such particulars can be furnished in due time, should, as I hope will be the case, they be wanted. It is as unfair to the respective peoples of India that they should be ruled by a centralized and distant authority, as it would be for France, Germany, Austria, Italy, Spain, *Comparison with Europe.* Portugal, Holland, Denmark, and Belgium, to become vassals of one monarch, and that monarch an Asiatic, compelling the adoption of Asiatic methods of rule.

Not the least conspicuous merit in Mr. Bright's proposal *Political self-reliance.* is that it would teach the Indian people political self-reliance. In scores of ways which no one can forecast, as no one can positively set forth the possible developments of the future, by granting them a measure of self-government the utmost conceivable service would be done for our Indian fellow-subjects. I can imagine no grander, no more noble, work for the National *The work to be done, one which the Federation may accomplish.* Liberal Federation than that it should make Justice for India one of its leading objects. Such a task as I have, in outline, indicated in the foregoing pages must some day be performed by one Association or another in this country if Englishmen are to show themselves worthy of their position and mindful of their duty to their fellow-subjects in the East. It is a task which, under the terrible peril of an awful harvest if neglected, must not be avoided. Our responsibilities in India are of our own seeking. Let us, as Englishmen, see to it that no desire for ease, no aversion to the trouble of familiarising ourselves with unfamiliar facts, no sneers from parties interested in maintaining the present system, turn us aside from at least attempting to do our duty.

No time could be more propitious for action than the *Present time propitious.* present, *i.e.*, regarding the affairs of both England and India on the whole. India is receiving at the hands of Mr. Gladstone's Government a measure of justice and consideration to which it has not been accustomed. After nearly two hundred years of a precisely opposite policy, Mr. Gladstone has inaugurated a new policy in making arrangements for this country to bear a portion of the cost of the recent Afghan wars. The people of England fully approve of what has been done, and are animated with the most friendly sentiments towards their fellow-subjects in the East. The occasion for forward action is ripe: the question is, Are we ready?

WM. DIGBY.

COROMANDEL, FORD PARK, MUTLEY,
    PLYMOUTH; *October*, 1881.

POSTSCRIPT.

SINCE this Letter was written, and while the pages are passing through the Press, information has been received from India of the issue of an important Minute by the Government. Only an outline of the document has yet reached this country, but enough has been published to give great force to the suggestions which I have made. On the line of Mr. Bright's proposals considerable progress has from time to time been made ; a further step has just been taken. It now remains for English electoral opinion, exerted through the House of Commons, to take care that with the partial decentralization of finance shall proceed thorough decentralization in other respects. The Governor-General in Council hopes that the extension of the scheme for the decentralization of the finances will develop local self-government. To this end the Provincial Governments are instructed to make a careful scrutiny of their accounts, with a view of ascertaining what items of receipt and charge can be transferred from the provincial to the local heads for administration *by a committee comprising non-official and, wherever possible, elected members*, and also what measures are necessary for the purposes of introducing more local self-government, equalizing local and municipal taxation throughout the Empire, checking severe or unsuitable imposts, and favouring forms most accordant with the popular opinion or sentiment. Then follow details regarding the treatment of the principal heads of the receipts and charges, the general result being that nearly three-fifths of the revenue and about one-fourth of the expenditure of British India will be provincialized.

The *Gazette of India*, in giving details of this policy, says that in the first place it is proposed to apply to the whole of

[Marginal notes:] Decentralization of Finance. Local self-government. Indian Government suggesting elected members. Will of the people ascertained. Principles adopted.

Principle adopted. India the principle upon which the most recent settlement—namely, that with Burmah in 1879—was framed. That principle is that, instead of giving to the local Governments a fixed sum to make good any excess in the provincial expenditure over the provincial receipts, a certain proportion of the Imperial revenue of each province should be devoted to this object. Certain heads of the revenue will be reserved as Imperial, others divided between Imperial and provincial, and the rest made wholly provincial. The balance of the transfers being against the provinces will be rectified by assigning to each province a fixed percentage on its land revenue. In Bengal this will amount to 38 per cent.; in Madras, 26 per cent.; in Bombay, 50 per cent.; in the North-West Provinces, 22 per cent.; in the Panjab, 43 per cent.; in the Central Provinces, 48 per cent.; in Assam, 49 per cent.; and in Burmah, 33 per cent. It is hoped that the result of this system will be to give to the Provincial Governments a direct interest in the most important item of the Imperial revenue raised within their own province. Here, again, one of the principles laid down by Mr. Bright is made of service by the Indian Government of to-day. Where so much has been granted more may be obtained.

Increased responsibility of Provincial Governments. Following the above, is a proposal which is of the highest importance. More responsibility is to be thrown upon the Provincial Governments than they now possess. It would be cruel to the Indian people to grant this additional responsibility to the Provincial authorities, and allow it to be held in the alien hands which have not done wisely and well with the power they already possess. It is intended by the Viceroy's Minute to modify the existing arrangements Financial Autonomy. between the Imperial and Provincial Governments regarding the resources granted in the event of fiscal misfortune, such as a heavy loss on the Opium revenue, or a national disaster, such as a war or a severe famine. It is declared, on the one hand, that the local Governments must look for no special aid except in case of severe famine, and then only within certain limits; and, on the other hand, that the Imperial Government will make no demand on them except in case of a disaster so abnormal as to exhaust the Imperial reserves and necessitate the suspension of the entire machinery of public improvement. Aid will be given to the provinces in a severe famine only if the current provincial income during the period of the distress has been exhausted, and if the accumulated savings of the past years, in excess of the ordinary working balance, have been drawn upon to the extent of two-thirds of the total amount. The margin of the provincial income over the expenditure in normal years will be made liable for the completion of the relief works begun during the famine, or will be chargeable to the extent of one-fourth for the payment of the interest on the Imperial loans contracted to meet the cost of the famine. The Imperial Government expresses the hope that if a sufficient surplus accrues at the close of the current financial year it may be able to restore to the Provincial Governments the contributions, aggregating sixty-seven lakhs (£670,000), made by them for the Afghan war, on the receipt of satisfactory assurances that these amounts will be devoted to productive public works. I am indebted for the summary of this important Minute to *The Times'* Indian telegram of October 10th.

Provinces to meet their own calamities.

When I began my Letter, nothing beyond the conspicuous act of justice which Mr. Gladstone has performed in respect to the Afghan war expenditure justified me in employing the present time for urging the importance of Indian affairs upon my countrymen. But, before my pleadings have an opportunity of meeting the eyes of those to whom they are addressed, the most appropriate of all occasions for forward and vigorous action in this country has revealed itself. While, on the one hand, there is no time to be lost, on the other there is sufficient time to concert means, and upon those means to take action in next session of Parliament. All that is done in the Viceroy's Minute which is summarised above, is recommendatory. No actual step has been taken. The Provincial Governments are merely instructed to 'make enquiry.' Now, to carry out thoroughly

Appropriateness of present time for action.

Viceroy's Minute recommendatory only

the spirit of the new proposals, and make them what Mr. Bright suggested in his '58 speeches, and also to make them really effective for good, English effort is needed. It would be too much to expect from human nature—at least, from Anglo-Indian official human nature, which is sensitive to criticism to an abnormal degree—that the Provincial Governments of India will report favourably of a proposal which will place their every act under scrutiny, and render every officer in their employ amenable to public criticism, and, it may be, to rebuke not merely in the newspaper Press, but in a partially-elective Assembly also. If Lord Ripon's Minute is to do any good, it must be supplemented by earnest action in Great Britain, and by special efforts in the House of Commons, which is now the controlling power in Indian affairs. When officials in the position of the Viceroy of India and his Council go so far as to admit that the people of India have the right to a voice in the administration of nearly three-fifths of the revenue, and about one-fourth of the expenditure, of their country, it is clear that the need for reform is very pressing. None in this country know better than the members of the National Liberal Federation how slow heads of departments and permanent officials, save in very exceptional instances, are to confess that things could possibly be better than they are at any given moment. Outside agitation is always needed in Great Britain to initiate reform, and to make beneficial change possible. The same thing is true, in a hundred-fold degree, as regards India, of any real and substantial reform. But, as I have shown in the preceding pages, agitation there is practically unknown, and is not to be too readily encouraged. More may be done by judicious and amply-instructed effort in England than possibly could be done in India.

I venture to hope that, at this crisis, when an unexpected tendency towards Liberalising the institutions of India is exhibited by the Indian Government, English aid will not be wanting. If properly dealt with, the Minute issued at Calcutta on the 8th October may be found to constitute a new Charter

English assistance needed.

of the liberties of the people of India. Hitherto the political organizations of this country have existed for purposes almost, if not entirely, personal to the inhabitants of Great Britain. If it should prove that the National Liberal Federation is prepared to enter upon duties involving not a little self-sacrifice, bringing no reward to the workers therein save the consciousness of the right course having been attempted, but having as their ultimate result the benefiting of the hundreds of millions of the people of India, it will be made clear that the sense of public duty in the present day has been lifted to a higher level than usual, and that the standard of English political character is nobler than it has hitherto been. Should my anticipations prove correct, the new Minute on Indian Financial Decentralization will, through English effort have issues undreamt of by the Council of Notables who sent it forth.—W. D.